"The Gilly"

A Flyfisher's Guide to British Columbia

ISBN 0–88925–638–1

Published by
Alf Davy
Box 1738
Kelowna, B.C.
Canada

Published for British Columbia Flyfishers with all money going to British Columbia Flyfishers Conservation Fund.

First printing, 1985

Printed and bound in Canada by
Friesen Printers
a Division of D. W. Friesen & Sons Ltd.
Altona, Manitoba R0G 0B0
Canada

"The Gilly"
A Flyfisher's Guide to British Columbia

Compiled and Edited by
Alfred G. Davy

This book is dedicated to my father, Alf Davy, who taught me a love of fishing, my wife, Verneta, who allows me to pursue it and my children, Valia and Ayra, who I hope will have a place to pursue it.

Alfred G. Davy

"The curious thing about fishing is you never want to go home. If you catch anything, you can't stop. If you don't catch anything, you hate to leave in case something might bite."

Gladys Taber
Ladies' Home Journal (1941)

'Gilly' — A historical fishing term to describe a guide who accompanies and helps an angler to fish.

Acknowledgements

Special thanks to the contributors of this publication. They are non–professional writers who have given of their time and experience to help others become better flyfishers. Their collective experience extends over 400 years.

Doug Porter	Tim Tullis	Mike Maxwell
Jim Crawford	Brian Chan	Barry Thornton
Denise Maxwell	Ralph Shaw	Tom Murray
Alf Davy	Ehor Boyanowsky	Peter Caverhill

I am grateful to Jim Crawford without whose help this book would not have been as well done; to Steve Carter for his fine free hand drawings and to Verneta Davy for all the help with rereads and rewrites.

The book is jointly funded by the British Columbia Federation of Flyfishers, the editor Alfred G. Davy and some of the writers. Profits from the book will be used for the enhancement and conservation of fishing in British Columbia.

Front Cover: Sunrise on Hatheume Lake by Tim Tullis

Back Cover: Top — 9 lb. rainbow that was photographed and released. by Alf Davy

Bottom — Bulkley Steelhead by Trevor Venables

Fly Photographs: Jim Crawford

The "Gilly"

A Flyfisher's Guide to British Columbia

Foreword

    I have taught fly fishing, casting and fly tying for the past fifteen years and have come to realise it is a sport which very few master completely. Some make a start by trolling flies, but the majority of fishermen do not fly fish. Observe how many people are casting flies the next time you are fishing.

    Today there is a real need for all fishermen to change their attitudes and become concerned about conservation. Tremendous pressure is being put on our fishing resources because of easy access to water by industrial roads. However, government agencies and conservation groups have introduced more restrictions on fishing: it is no longer acceptable to catch as many fish as possible or to kill the entire catch. Those interested in preserving our fishing heritage want to see more of the current regulations *enforced* . . . especially for numbers, size of fish and gear restrictions.

    Many of us enjoy fishing with family and friends, and certainly everyone likes to have some chance of success. But a method of fishing should not be taken away without giving something in return and I hope the ''Gilly'' is that something.

    How do you help a beginning fly fisher? The obvious way

would be to take them out fishing and show them how it's done — to be a guide or gilly, that is a person who can help them become more proficient.

First, though, you must examine your attitude towards fishing. Everyone seems to go through the same various stages: wanting to catch the most fish, then the largest fish, then the most difficult fish. Finally the fisherman learns to relax and just enjoy the sport, nature and companionship it can bring. Then comes a reluctance on the part of any fisherman to tell too much. He realizes if everyone is able to catch fish too easily, our natural resource will not be able to stand the pressure and we will all be the poorer for it.

We hear stories about the old days of how sacks of fish were caught. Where I grew up in Terrace on the Skeena River, there was one individual in the early 1960's who used to come up each summer and fish the Kitimat, Skeena, and Kalum Rivers. One summer, he landed and killed fifty-four Spring Tyee salmon with an average weight of forty-three pounds. He lived alone in his camper and gave the fish away to whoever happened to be around. Because of the over fishing, that particular section around Terrace now has special restrictions with closures in August. But there are still many instances of such excesses even today, such as the canning of Rainbow trout in the Interior of B.C. and salmon on the coast. Certainly, good common sense and a better understanding of conservation is needed for the future.

It is hoped that along with some lessons on *how* to fly fish, the "Gilly" will give the reader the essence of *why* to fly fish — to reach a level of fishing that is in harmony with nature for our enjoyment now and for generations to come. Certainly to catch a few fish for eating is part of the enjoyment but also to look at each fish, to be aware you are taking it and to be thankful for the gift, is another part. In the old days you could take all the fish you wanted. For the present, we must only take some. For the future, we may not be able to take any unless we make the appropriate attitude changes now.

Alfred G Davy.

I
Where to Fish Lakes and When to Change Flies

by Doug Porter

Two questions I am often asked while instructing students in fly tying are "where do you fish in an unfamiliar lake?" and "when do you change flies?". Since fly tying and entomology (study of insects) are inseparable components of the larger whole of fly fishing, I blend them throughout the course, mixed well with lines, leaders, retrieves, and strategies.

"Did ya hear about "Secret Lake"? Someone says they're catching fish to 10 lbs. on a dry fly! Whatta ya say we go there next week and give'er a try?" Now there was an opportunity I seldom passed up; a chance to fish new waters in relentless pursuit of the fabled angling mecca. Many of my early expeditions to such a lake, newly rediscovered following a stocking program by the Fish & Wildlife Branch, ended in disappointment and frustration. My high expectations weren't shattered from a lack of effort, but from an inability to read the water and understand aquatic life. Since entomology is covered elsewhere in this book by a professional, let's concentrate on the subject of where to start when fishing an unfamiliar lake.

The Lake
Assuming you've done your sleuthing and received

1

accurate instructions on how to get to "Secret Lake", you and your fishing partner arrive early to find no one else around on this particular weekday. The small lake is placid in the morning sun with not a ripple from wind or fish. Without further hesitation the boat is launched into this unfamiliar environment. If someone else had been anchored on the lake, you could always discreetly row up to the edge of the invisible 100 foot territorial perimeter that has been previously staked (which etiquette dictates unless invited), and ask how the fishing is. Since this opportunity doesn't exist, you must read the water!

How do you find the fish? Some advice that was given to me years ago was to slowly troll a Doc Spratley wet fly on a sinking line until I caught a trout, then make note of where I caught it, and examine the stomach contents. This was a profound piece of advice that worked well in my developmental years, but had long since been replaced with a combination of growing knowledge and fly fishing experience.

What I have learned is to explore a lake to become familiar with its changing shoreline and depths, as well as the type of bottom it has. The location of fish in any lake is dependent on a number of inter-related influences which will now be explored.

Setting

To gain a better understanding of "Secret Lake", let's place it in the Interior of B.C. at an elevation of 1800 m (5500 ft.) above sea level. At that elevation we know that it is subject to being iced over for up to 6 months of the year. It has no inlet or outlet stream, and its level is maintained by seepage and run-off water. To really appreciate "Secret Lake", or any lake for that matter, we have to view it as a unique ecosystem. An evolved plant and animal community adapted to and coexisting within this particular environment.

Factors Affecting a Lake

A natural balance is maintained throughout the food chain dictated by the availability of nutrients, for both plant or animal, from the simplest single-celled organisms through the most complex. Most life forms require sunlight, so the depth to which it penetrates is where most of these organisms can be found busily going about surviving. A mud or marl bottom offers the most favorable location for plant and animal communities to develop as nutrients are more available there than on a rock or sand bottom. This doesn't imply that there is no life in rocky or sandy areas, but that it is likely to be far more abundant where living conditions are more favourable.

Water temperature is important in influencing growth and retaining oxygen. Most deep lakes (over 35') stratify into three layers, with the most dense layer (coldest) at the bottom, a mid layer varying in temperature, and the upper layer being warmest. (This is the normal situation during most of the ice-free period). Since oxygen concentrations are highest in colder water, organisms requiring large amounts of oxygen will seek conditions which best accommodate their needs. In the case of rainbow trout, their preference is 59° (15°C) temperature with at least 5 parts per million of oxygen. Incidently, oxygen can enter a lake in many ways: through surface exchange interaction with the air, through plant respiration, from stream water, and through springs.

Sunlight influences both oxygen processes of surface exchange and plant respiration. Plants require sunlight to carry on photosynthesis, of which oxygen is a by-product (also water clarity determines the depth of sunlight penetration, hence the depth at which plants can survive), while the surface temperature determines the amount of oxygen transfer taking place. The warmer and calmer the water, the less oxygen it will receive through contact with the air.

The time of day also influences insect movement. While sunlight warms the water to temperatures required to trigger emergences (hatches), it also inhibits insect movement during the time of day when its rays penetrate the deepest. Aquatic insects are most active during periods of low light, and many are nocturnal.

As discussed earlier, wind is important in the oxygen transfer process by creating more water surface to contact the air. It also enables water to circulate in the upper layer. This circulation creates a current which can move aquatic insects away from the shoreline toward deeper water, or move insects on the surface toward the shoreline.

The combined action of wind and sun, throughout the early spring and summer, can cause the upper level of a lake to warm to a temperature which fish can't tolerate. This usually occurs by August, and lasts into September when the surface begins to cool as the nights get colder and longer. The inactivity of the trout at this time is referred to as the ''summer doldrums'' and can explain the apparent absence of fish.

The clearness of water is the product of the materials that are dissolved in it. As a generality, degrees of acidity determines the depth to which sunlight penetrates, consequently the littoral zone is where most life will congregate. Alkaline water (pH more than 7) is clear with sunlight penetration up to 40–50 feet, while acidic water (pH less than 7) is usually darker with considerably less sunlight penetration, a shallower limnetic zone, generally cooler water temperatures, and shorter periods subject to the doldrums.

Elevation is also a key to a lake's productivity and fishability, relative to its ice–free period. Lower elevation lakes are usually more productive since they are ice–free longer, but are subject to warm surface water periods proportionately. High elevation lakes tend to be less productive, food–wise, but aren't usually affected by summer doldrums, as their ice–free period isn't long enough and the nights generally cool enough to maintain colder temperatures.

The reader should by now appreciate that this brief description of most of the factors influencing trout behaviour is just that, brief. I might also add that fish are for the most part, sensitive to pollution, especially the noise type; banging in boats, racing motors, splashing anchors, flitting shadows, and even fly lines.

Fishing the Lake

Let's now apply what we've learned to "Secret Lake". Going back to the beginning, we had heard these large fish were taking dry flies. Allowing for third party exaggeration, we'll assume the fish probably average 3–5 lbs., not ten (possible, but not likely). We can further surmise that the fish were taking sedges (caddisflies) since this is the last part of June.

Since it is still early in the morning, there is plenty of time to row around the edge of the lake and make note of bottom types, drop–offs, weed beds, and rock outcrops, while searching for underwater insect activity and foraging fish. Map it! Next, take a few passes over the middle parts of the lake, dropping an anchor occasionally to test the depth. (Don't forget to troll your Knouff Lake Special sedge pupae pattern while doing this).

Make note of prominent shoreline features on both sides of the lake to use as reference points for your probe lines while depth sounding. Pay particular attention as your anchor reaches bottom to the amount of resistance. If it hits solidly, expect rock or gravel, while if it settles some, there is probably a mud or marl bottom. Some residue will also usually cling to your anchor when it's brought up.

Once you have satisfied yourself that you have a good mental picture of the lake's underwater structure, you must decide whether to fish along the drop–offs where weeds are

4

abundant, or in the deeper water with a mud bottom. If no fish were seen in the shallower water, my choice would be to anchor in the shallows first, and cast over the drop-off area in hopes of intercepting a cruising fish, while watching for signs of insect and fish activity. If this didn't produce results using a chironomid or Knouff Lake Special on a floating line and long 6-20' (5-6m.) leader, I would move out over the mud bottom area less than 40 feet [12m.] of water and switch to a medium or fast sinking line and use the same flies.

Fish Food

Taking a moment to reflect back on the crash course in lake environments just covered, most of the same factors which affect it also determine what fly will likely produce the best. Your success then is at best conditional, relative to your ability to interpret what is happening in the aquatic world and adapting to the constantly changing activities of the insects, through presentation and imitation. These aquatic insects can be broken down into two broad categories, those that spend their entire lives in the lake, and those which enjoy a brief respite from the water during their adult stages.

Included in the first category are shrimp, leeches, snails, and the lesser organisms such as the copepods and daphnia, as well as various water beetles and corixa backswimmers (though these last two have the ability to fly, and do so in spring and fall).

The second group consists of insects which go through a transition from the nymphal or pupal stage which is aquatic, to an adult stage which is terrestrial. They include dragon and damsel flies, mayflies, caddisflies (sedges), and the multitudinous genus and species of insects in the order diptera such as chironomids, mosquitos, blackflies, and chaoborus collectively referred to as midges. While this list is by no means complete, it does represent the largest bulk of trout food sources in most lakes.

At any season you can expect fish to be feeding on the most abundant organism that is easily vulnerable to it. Again the environmental variables discussed earlier come into play. In the spring after ice-off, as the water temperature warms and the sunlight penetrates deeper, insects respond by becoming more active, triggering emergences starting in the shallower waters and progressing to the deeper waters throughout the spring and early summer. The trout respond to these emergences as they occur, keying or selecting that particular insect, and following it from bottom to top, for the duration of the emergence or hatch which may be as short as

5

one hour, or occur at a given time over many days. Diptera species differ uniquely in that they emerge for the entire period that the lake is ice-free. Damsel fly and dragon fly nymphs also differ as they migrate shoreward before climbing out and shucking their nymphal skins.

During the lull between hatchs or migrations, trout will forage for food where oxygen levels and water temperatures are suitable. In lakes where shrimp are found then, this would mean a return to feeding on shrimp and picking up whatever other aquatics it happened across during its feeding periods.

Changing Flies

Now let's go back to "Secret Lake". Time passes as you continue casting your Knouff Lake Special along the drop-off next to a rock outcropping. Varying your retrieve from slow pulls to short jerks finally produces a nice fish of 2 lbs. (1 kg.) After landing the fish and spooning the stomach contents, you find a mixture of the remnants of shrimp, chironomids, and one dragonfly nymph, along with two sedge pupae which are still alive. Obviously the fish was feeding on shrimp much earlier before turning to the diptera species. Now it appears that it was starting to key to the sedge pupae as they begin their swim to the surface. If the hatch is large enough to attract a few fish, the promise of some excellent fishing is forecast. Two more fish are landed and released, the largest weighing 4 lbs.

Soon, adult sedges are observed drifting on the surface, moved by the slight breeze which has recently come up. As you watch them float by, you anticipate the splashy rise of feeding trout, indicative of a sedge being taken off the surface. Nothing. You continue taking fish on the pupal imitation for a few more casts when you are suddenly startled by a loud splash behind you. You turn in time to see large concentric rings ebbing toward your boat. Quickly you reel in your sinking line and switch to your dry line. Shortening your leader length to ten or twelve feet from the longer one used for chironomids, you tie on a Tom Thumb, enjoying moderate success for the duration of the emergence, moving your boat once as the hatch shifted from your original location.

All too soon it is over, as the last sedge flies for the safety of the trees. It is now 1:30, still lots of fishing time left. The Tom Thumb produces a couple more half-hearted rises, but no fish. Returning to the wet line and pupae produces another fish, but the action has slowed to a standstill. Surface movement on the far side of the lake attracts your attention. Rowing over, you find a few large chironomid pupae cases on

6

the surface. The water is twenty feet deep with a mud bottom. Switching again to your dry line and a long leader, you tie on a half–back, cast it out quartering with the breeze, and let it drift with the wind (dead drift). A couple of fish later, you decide it's time to head back home after a rewarding day of fishing, taking with you memories of leaping trout, a map of a new lake, and wondering thoughts at the possibilities of there really being 10 lb. trout in this peaceful little body of water.

When to change flies then is not so much guess work as it is responding to the changing attitudes of the feeding fish. There will always be times when fish are not feeding, or are feeding so heavily that any fly presented in any fashion will take them. Knowing the environment, the insects found there, and their life cycles are just a few of the things one needs to know to become moderately successful. As for those days when nothing seems to work and the fish are irresponsive even when everything else seems to indicate a good day for fishing — well, that's part of the ultimate challenge of the sport, keeping it interesting enough to occupy my time for the rest of my life.

THE TROUT FISHERS' BAG

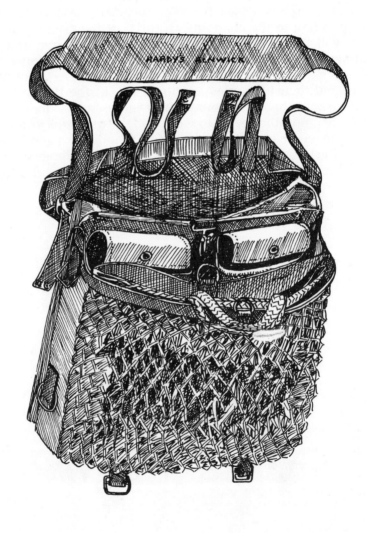

II
Equipment Basics
by Jim Crawford

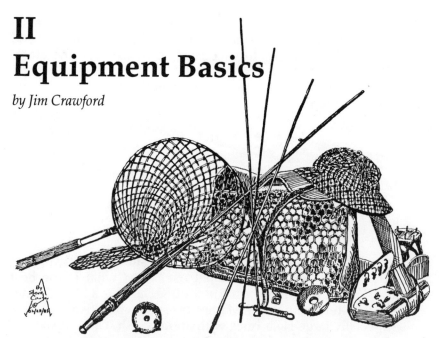

British Columbia is indeed a fisherman's paradise! We are blessed with an almost overwhelming abundance of quality trout lakes and streams, steelhead rivers, and saltwater habitat, all of which provide outstanding opportunities — especially for fly fishers. Needless to say, with such a wide range of fishing environments, choice of equipment could become complicated, and any thorough discussions would take far more time than we have available. So we will limit this to fly equipment most useful on *lakes* since that is what B.C. has most of . . .

It's fair to say most equipment used for stillwater flyfishing is also suitable for moving waters, the major exception being steelhead or salmon in "heavy" rivers. Saltwater and estuary fishing for cutthroat or salmon also requires special corrosion–resistant equipment. But generally, and allowing for perhaps some slight bias by the writer, equipment described here will be useful in the majority of situations.

It is important to understand that in lakes, trout are constantly on the move looking for food (compared to streams where they take up stations and food comes to them). Down in the distortion–free stillwater environment fish can leisurely observe their food forms, which means the fly fisher must take great care: fly patterns must be near–perfect, leaders must be unobstrusive, and presentation with the proper equipment is crucial.

Fly fishing — that is — actually casting a fly, is not at all difficult *if* the fly fisher has "balanced" equipment . . . and that is really the key to success. Our discussion, therefore, will include fly rods, reels, lines, and to a lesser degree, leaders, and the fine harmony or balance that must be created between them.

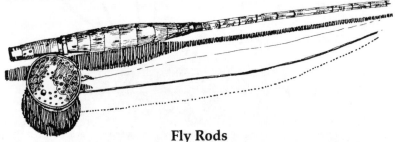

Fly Rods

Probably the most often asked question about fly fishing other than "what fly should I use?" is "what is the best rod?". In a word, the best rod for B.C. lakes is a "long" one, eight to ten feet. Why? Mainly because when fishing lakes, especially large clear ones with spooky fish, casts of sixty or eighty feet are fairly common and quite simply, long rods make casting easier. They also allow more room for correcting mistakes during the cast.

But I must qualify that by also saying long–rod fishing has only recently become enjoyable with the advent of *graph–ite* and its light weight and superb casting qualities. Up to that time hand–crafted bamboo fly rods were considered "best", more because of aesthetics than anything else I think . . . though avid split cane fans stubbornly defend against all "modern" rod materials including fiberglass, graphite, and boron. A full day of casting each would quickly make converts to the lighter–weight graphite rods, I'm sure. However, we aren't here to pass judgement on that aspect.

Without question the most dramatic changes in fly fishing equipment have occurred with rods. After bamboo came fiberglass, the first man–made material to be adapted to mass production of rods. Probably eighty percent of all fly fishers own or have owned a fiberglass flyrod. Close behind is graphite, a true "space–age" material. So popular has graphite become in its short history (since about 1970), I'm certain it will soon overtake glass as the predominant rod material . . . especially as prices go down.

Which brings us back to the main point . . . Like everything else, there really isn't any one rod which will be "best" for all conditions. If you are an average fly fisher you will ultimately own about three rods: one for big waters, one or two for everyday fishing, and perhaps one little fun rod for brushy streams and small lakes.

Fly rods are built to cast specific weight fly lines. Fortunately for us the American Fishing Tackle Manufacturers Association (AFTMA) developed a simple numerical weight system for fly rods and lines so they could be easily matched or balanced together by number. A chart of weights assigned to those numbers is shown at the end of the following section on **Fly Lines** for it is actually a portion of the line which is weighed. Fly rods are then assigned a number describing the line weight they cast best. Rated #1 to #15 — bigger is heavier, with #6 or #7 being about average for most fishing in our country.

The rod I personally use more than any other for fishing B.C. trout lakes is a nine foot graphite rated for 5-6 weight lines. I also use a nine and one-half foot rod rated for 6-7 lines when I fish big lakes down deep, and a little seven footer that handles 3-4 weight lines. As obvious as the comment may be, which rod to use really depends on the situation. And contrary to what may be said elsewhere, physical strength of the caster *is* a factor when choosing a rod. For example, a small person may easily handle a ten foot rod with an 8 or 9 weight line and make sixty or seventy foot casts . . . for awhile! Casting that rod for a couple of hours will almost guarantee extreme pain in wrist and forearm. But give that same person a well-balanced eight foot rod rated for a 6-7 weight line and they will cast just as far (because of increased line speed with the shorter rod), and be far less fatigued at the end of the day. Stronger athletic-type persons may well be able to handle a big rod — heavy line system all day. But most of us can't. Choose a bit lighter outfit to begin and graduate to heavier systems as your own dimensions of fly fishing expand.

Another major consideration when choosing a rod is "softness" or flex. That is largely determined by the line weight it is built for, but it also depends on the rod "design". Some rods are designed to flex clear down into the handle; others only at the tip. It becomes a matter of personal preference . . . some people preferring the wet-noodle effect, others including myself, preferring a bit crisper action.

The type of fishing you like to do will be a determining factor also . . . For example, in B.C. we do a lot of dry (floating) line nymph fishing with small flies and long, light leaders. I tend to get excited when fish hit, and I often set the hook more vigorously than I should. A heavy line rod or stiff action

11

rod would break the leader every time, even on small fish. But the rod I use for that type of fishing has a very soft, forgiving tip action and its stiffness or casting power is down in the butt section.

Fishing deep water with a full sinking line is something else again . . . There is no question that long, stiff rods are better for lifting a dense sinking line up out of the water and keeping it airborne while casting. But you sacrifice feel and "forgiveness" with a rod like that. It is better to stay with the softer tip rod and learn to pick up less line than switch to a stiff action rod. Your casting distance may suffer a bit but you will break off far fewer fish.

Obviously we could go on and on about different situations and rods to match, but the point is made: whether it is bamboo, fiberglass, graphite or whatever, there is no one "best" rod for everyone. Try as many different rods as possible, talk to other fly fishers, attend casting clinics, then settle on the rod action that feels best for you.

In addition to rod lengths, materials, and actions, rod hardware is also a consideration. Beginning with the handle or grip, specific materials are used for a reason. Most grips are constructed of cork. Good dense cork will last almost forever. It is soft, sensitive, flexible, and easily shaped and repaired. Soft rubber or composite grips are okay, but do not allow any "contact" with the rod. They are easy on the hand but tend to twist under pressure and are not suited to fly rods.

Shape of the grip is a personal thing. The most common in our area are the western or straight grip, the cigar or tapered grip, and the midge or sharp taper grip. The midge grip is usually found on tiny light weight rods, and the other two on more powerful rods. There is probably no real advantage of one over another, except perhaps the western grip with its slightly raised center and flared front section allows more power to be applied during casting.

Reel seats are not really a big deal. Many expensive rods have corrosion-resistant reel seats and exotic wood spacers on which the reel itself seats, but other than good looks there is no advantage over plain aluminum seats of the same design. Big-game rods for tarpon, billfish or other ocean giants require strong reel seats for the heavy reels used . . . and the abuse . . . but in our kind of fishing we don't have to consider that.

Some small rods, particularly those used on small eastern streams, have two sliding rings that fit snugly over the reel foot. Made for very light weight reels, these are not especially useful on the equipment we normally use here in B.C.

Line guides of "eyes" are a rather important topic. So much has been written and said about such a seemingly insignificant thing that we must discuss it, though we only have room to touch on it briefly.

Most rods today are two-piece with a lower "butt-section" and upper "tip section." There are also specialty rods with three, four and even six sections, but for normal use, two-piece rods will be most common. The large circular guides on the butt section are called stripping guides, and flatter wire guides on the tip section are snake guides. Some rods have stripping-type guides of varying sizes throughout their length and on the tip-top . . . We will discuss the advantages and disadvantages a bit later.

Guides, believe it or not, are as responsible for smooth, accurate line delivery as the rod! Many thousands of man-hours and computer-hours have been spent by rod builders developing guide spacing formulas based on rod lengths, materials and actions. With the advent of graphite an entirely new concept had to be dealt with: high line speeds created extreme friction and heat and guide materials to handle that had to be adapted. Softer metal guides previously used on bamboo and glass rods would quickly wear through on graphite rods, so harder chromium steel and tungsten carbide stripping guides and tip-tops were developed. Those didn't wear, but they created so much heat through line friction during casting that coatings on fly lines cracked. The next generation of stripping guides utilized "ceramics" (space-age plastics) and teflons, and the flyline manufacturers created more durable coatings, so that we now have rods *and* lines which respond beautifully to the casting quality demanded by graphite rod fly fishers. Cane rod and fiberglass advocates have also benefitted from those developments.

If you look closely at fly rods in sporting goods stores or equipment catalogs you'll notice the vast majority are made with one or two stripping guides on the butt section, snake guides along the tip section, and a single wire loop fly rod tip-top. There is sound reasoning for that: fly lines are heavy and have very large diameters compared to monofilament and other casting lines. Remember, we must use a thick fly line for its weight which is needed to propel the fly. As the line shoots through the guides it tends to bunch up and drag because of its larger surface area and weight. The first guide will be a larger diameter stripping guide, used much the same as a spinning rod guide to catch the line and funnel it on to the next guide. The fine wire snake guides help reduce friction as the line flattens out and shoots. On big powerful rods there may be as many as three stripping guides, but extensive tests by rod companies like Fenwick and Orvis, and line companies such as Cortland and Scientific Angler have proven that the more stripping guides there are the more friction and drag is generated. The current fad among many custom and do-it-yourself fly rod builders of putting singlefoot stripping-type guides along the entire length of their rods actually inhibits casting distance if conventional fly lines are used. Those rods were developed specifically for shooting heads with mono-filament line or fine diameter running lines where extreme line speeds are generated. Even the tip-top makes a big difference. Ceramic tops have been shown to cause up to 25% more drag on fly lines compared to wire loop tip-tops! So consider those things when choosing a rod or having one built . . . Line guides do indeed play an important part in how well and how far you cast.

There is a mountain more of information available on fly rods, especially as we get into special purpose rods. But that comes later as we master what is currently before us. Now on to lines and reels . . .

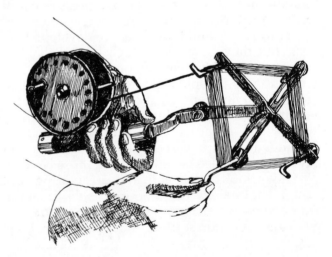

Fly Lines   THE LINE DRIER

Not too many years ago fly fishers only had to worry about *one* simple braided fly line of silk which served a dual purpose: with a good cleaning and some grease, it floated; if it was dirty or stripped of floatant, it sank! Sometime after WW

II nylon and dacron were developed into fly lines, but because each had its own specific gravity they performed differently on the same rod. Since all line markings to that time were based on the weight or specific gravity of silk lines, it was soon obvious that a new system or standard of weighing fly lines had to be developed.

As mentioned in our section on *rods* there is an organization called the American Fishing Tackle Manufacturers Association (AFTMA) which was formed expressly for the purpose of bringing uniformity and consistency within the fishing tackle industry. For fly fishing, categories were created for the different designs of fly lines and a numerical system assigned for judging the weights of fly lines and the rods to handle them.

There are currently three major fly line manufacturers: Berkeley, Cortland, and 3M–Scientific Anglers; three lesser known, Garcia, Gladding, and Sunset and probably several others. In addition there are many private label lines made by the main manufacturers. Unfortunately, all line makers use their own terminology to describe functions of their lines, so it is still somewhat confusing. But at least we do have a standard numerical system to classify line weights.

We can divide our discussion about fly lines into three categories: line design or *tapers*, line *function*, and line *weight*. Every fly line has *all three* components — taper, function and weight. Taper tells how the line is supposed to act when cast; function tells whether it is supposed to float or sink; and weight is based on grains of weight for that given line (shown by the number assigned).

In general there are seven *tapers* of fly lines: *Level Line* (L) — which has the same diameter from end to end and is used where presentation or long casts are not too essential. *Double Taper* (DT) — a long level diameter center section which gradually tapers down at both ends. Used primarily for delicate presentations and roll casts, and is not recommended for distance casting. Ends may be reversed on the reel for economy when one end wears out. *Weight Forward* (WF) — designed with more weight in the forward section, a quicker front taper than the DT and a long smaller diameter running line which "shoots" through guides for long casts. Undoubtedly the most used line on our B.C. lakes. Also known as a "torpedo" taper or "rocket" taper. *Bug Taper* (WF) — a weight forward with an even shorter front taper designed for casting heavy, wind resistant flies. Also called a "bass" bug taper, or "blunt tip". *Salt Water* (WF) — Very similar to the

15

bug taper but made with a very fine diameter running line for even longer casts; generally available only in heavy line weights. *Shooting Heads* (ST) — Exclusively for long distance casting where presentation is not a criterion, and designed with an attaching loop for quick changes (i.e.: from slow sink to super fast sink, or to floating). Only about 30 ft. in length, shooting tapers correspond in shape and weight to the forward 30 ft. of a full WF line, but attach with a loop to a running or shooting line of special design (such as a very fine diameter level line or monofilament). *Shooting Line* (SL) — a relatively new type of level line which has a very fine diameter and a hard coating which allows it to "shoot" through your guides with a minimum of resistance. This line is made specifically for use with shooting heads.

Okay, that is a description of line *tapers* available. The next part of this discussion has to do with line *function* . . . what does a line do? Basically, fly lines are made to float or sink.

All manufacturers produce lines which *float* — all pretty well I might add (with proper care), and lines which *sink*. All of my dry line fishing is done with weight forward (WF) lines which *must* "shoot" with the graphite rods I use. Virtually all fly lines are now made from non-stretch dacron, coated with special plastics to make them float or special "dense" coatings of plastic to make them sink. Graphite rods fire fly lines so fast that new harder outer coatings had to be developed. These new lines are really super for casting long distances as they really dance through the guides with a minimum of friction. Floating lines are found in all seven of the *tapers* mentioned (Level, DT, WF, etc.)

Sinking lines on the other hand are a bit more complicated. It is estimated that over 90% of the food available to fish is sub-surface, so it stands to reason the majority of our fishing should take place in that region. Fortunately the line companies agree and have come to our aid with an almost bewildering assortment of sinking lines. In fact, you may have to reread this to sort out what we're trying to say . . .

In addition to numerical line weights, sinking lines are also rated by how fast they sink (sink rate). Although called everything from neutral sink to super-extra-fast sink, for our purposes we can classify them into five categories: very slow, slow, medium, fast, and extra fast.

There is also one additional category which could be considered: the very specialized high density shooting line

made with a lead core, which in addition to being very difficult to cast, can be *very* dangerous at high speed.

The first group, the *very slows*, are currently available
only from major fly line companies in WF and DT. Rated as
"O" or neutral density lines, they operate from the surface
film down to about five feet, or a bit deeper on extremely slow
retrieves. As an avid surface strata nymph fisherman, I find
the very slow sink line fantastic on windy days because there
is little or no line bellying when fishing cross-wind.

The *slow sinks*, rated as TYPE-1 sinking lines, are useful
from five feet down to about ten feet below surface. This is
probably the most versatile sinking line to use in our lakes
because you can fish shallow shoals and weed beds, yet go
down deeper by just relaxing and letting it go. It is available in
WF and DT from nearly all manufacturers.

Medium sinking lines are rated TYPE-2 (though called
"fast" sinking by some manufacturers), and allow you to fish
depths from ten feet down to twenty on long, slow retrieves.
All manufacturers offer this line in WF, DT, and some in ST. I
use a #2 full sinking line fairly often in deeper water as it
allows the slower retrieves necessary with leech and dragon
patterns.

The *fast group*, rated TYPE-3 (and sometimes called Hi-D
and "extra fast") are not as versatile as slower lines, but can
be used with success when fishing deep drop-offs down to
thirty feet and beyond.

And the *extra fast* group, not really rated by a number, are
called Hi Speed Hi-D, and Type 4-Super Fast. These are
specialized lines for use in *very* deep water or fast moving
rivers. Available in WF and ST only, this class of lines has also
proven excellent in salt water when using large wind resistant
flies, especially in shooting tapers! The density of these lines
really drives big flies once line speed is developed . . . It also
drives big people who drop their back casts as I once proved
when I tried to change direction in mid-cast with a 550 Grain
ST. That line hit me right between the shoulder blades at 100 +
MPH, and literally knocked me to my knees. It really hurt!

Now, taking our knowledge about *tapers* and melding
that with our knowledge of line *functions* as described brings
us to the final, and certainly the simplest category of all, *line
weights* (not to be confused with sink rates of sinking lines).

Choosing a line weight can be a sort of chicken and egg
proposition. If you are buying a complete new outfit — rod,
reel, line, etc. there is no problem: pick a rod you like which is
rated for the line weight you want to use, and buy lines to

balance it. On the other hand many of us already have a fly rod of some sort or another. Modern rods are labelled for line weights they will handle, but older rods, and inexpensive rods are not, and it may be a challenge to find the right line weight to balance it.

The same holds true if one has a line and wishes to buy a rod to use it with. Without question the problem most often experienced in teaching casting to beginning fly fishermen is an improperly balanced outfit . . . a line which is either too light or too heavy for the rod (or the other way around . . .).

In fly casting, the line is probably the most important part of your outfit. Without proper line weight even the very best rods made are reduced to mere sticks. When casting, the fly *line* provides the weight needed to load or bend your rod and propel your fly as compared to spin casting where the lure or lead provides the weight and "pulls" out the line.

Fly lines are numbered from 1 up to 15 and are determined by weighing the first 30 feet of the line in grains, with the larger numbers representing heavier weights. A #1 line will weigh approximately 60 grains; a #7 line, about 180 grains; and #15 a whopping 550 grains. When applied to a sink rate or line speed, bigger is definitely faster — that is, a heavier sinking line with the same sink rate i.e.: WF9S — *type 3* will sink faster than a WF6S — *type 3*. And a WF9F floating line will shoot out faster and farther than a WF6F.

All that's left now is to take your knowledge . . . and go fishing. Probably your first line will be a floating line, then you'll move into full sinking lines of various sinking rates. And finally, you'll want to explore specialty lines like sink tips, sink heads, wet bellies, etc., because sooner or later you will find yourself in a situation where neither the floating nor full sinking lines will be exactly right for what you want to do. Designed primarily for streams where line mending is crucial, weight forward (WF) floating/sinking (F/S) lines allow you to fish sub-surface with the forward 5, 10, 20, or 30 foot sinking section of line available in *all* the sinking densities; and with 10 foot tip sections in type 0, 1, 2 or 3 in DT lines. Until a few years ago the WF F/S lines were available in type 2 and 3 sinking densities only. Now they are available in NF neutral through extra-fast and have become very popular, especially here in the West.

F/S lines are not my favourites in lakes except when fishing the shallows and the wind comes up. I have then used WF F/S neutral sink lines with good success. You can still "see" the strike on the floating portion and there is less bellying of the line than with a full floater. In most wind situations however, I would probably choose a full sink WF–S neutral line over the F/S.

Another situation in which I sometimes use a F/S in lakes is when fishing deep drop offs. I have a WF9 F/S type 3 30 foot sink head which goes down deep, quick. I can put it down over a drop–off and crawl my deer hair nymph creations right through the weeds. Because the "floating" portion is a brighter color than the sinking section it allows me to see it far down (it doesn't float at all, however, because the weight of the sinking portion pulls it under). It also gives me an idea how much line and leader are left when I see the color change between the two sections.

One last word on sinking tips is to comment on the "bent–L" theory which claims that strikes are missed because the sink tip line bends at the float/sink joint. Experts with far greater experience than I laugh at that, and one has only to study his sink tip as it is retrieved to see that it is *just* a theory. I suspect light refraction had something to do with it. Consider this: if anything the "bent–L" theory should be applied to dry–line nymph fishing where the nymph hangs at a virtual right angle to the line on very slow retrieves! This is one of my *very* favorite methods of fishing and I can promise you I don't miss many strikes . . . that line has only to twitch. The same holds true for sink tips. Watch the line where it enters the water and you'll begin to know when fish suck in your nymph. Some different movement occurs, not as noticeable as with a full floating line, but your line will move. If you use a graphite rod you will also develop a sixth sense when fish hit as there are subtle vibrations transmitted up the line and through the rod.

And finally, the basic message here is this: It makes sense to be prepared with more than one line. Ultimately you will have dozens, perhaps hundreds of flies, and maybe three or four rods of different lengths and weights. For each line weight you use, I recommend a good floating line, a good type 1 full sink, maybe a type 3 and perhaps a WF–F/S type "O" neutral density which will give you good coverage for the majority of situations and provide you with lots of fishing enjoyment! On the other hand, if all this is just too confusing, buy yourself the best floating line available, a lot of leader, weight your flies a bit (except the floating ones of course), and nymph fish all the depths by adjusting length of leader. You'll need infinite patience, good casting skills, and a bit of luck, but it can be very gratifying!

Key

L = Level Line
DT = Double Taper Line
WF = Weight Forward Line (also includes Bug taper and Salt water tapers in heavier line weights)
ST = Shooting Head (30 ft. coil)
F = Floating Line
F/S = Floating/Sinking Line
S = Full Sink Line
0, 1, 2, 3, 4, = Sink Rate

AFTMA Line Weight Standards

Line #	Allowable Wt.	Range	In Grains (Forward 30 ft.)
1	54–66		
2	74–86	9	230–250
3	94–106	10	270–290
4	114–126	11	318–342
5	134–146	12	368–392
6	152–168	13	450
7	177–193	14	500
8	202–218	15	550

By
Steve
Carter
04/21/85

Fly Reels

I have heard it said that if it wasn't for the necessity of having to stow fly line and backing, reels wouldn't be missed very much . . . Well, that may be true when fishing where trout only grow to twelve inches or so, or when dapping flies for bluegills and perch. But consider the consequences of a 200 pound marlin racing across the water; or a 20 pound steelhead heading to the next pool 150 yards down river; or an 8 pound Kamloops that decides the middle of the lake is where he wants to be — The plain fact is, reels are a very important part of the fly fishing system and in some instances their quality will be the direct difference between success and failure.

In keeping with our discussion about equipment for use primarily in B.C., it can be said that reels suitable for lakes can also be used on most moving waters. Because many of our waters hold trout capable of taking considerable line out with a long run, any reel used should be able to hold an entire fly line plus at least 50 yards of 20 pound dacron. That immediately excludes little ultra-light reels and so-called automatic (spring and ratchets) reels, and leaves single action and multiplier reels. Multipliers are all right . . . they have special gearing which allows reeling-in at a rate faster than 1:1. Each turn of the handle drives the line spool at a higher ratio due to gearing. I personally do not use multiplier reels because the gears create additional tension on the leader as a fish pulls line off the spool during a run. For most situations — and in fact I can't think of any where this won't be true — a good quality single action reel with handle directly fixed to the spool is totally adequate.

Two other considerations are quality and drag system. Virtually all name brand reels are of good quality . . . and price is not necessarily the important criterion. Most reels today are aluminum, either cast with alloys or machined from solid stock. Obviously the more expensive ones will be machine-cut from solid pieces then anodized or plated for corrosion resistance. Those are undoubtedly going to be fine quality, but so are many of the cast aluminum reels. And some old reels, especially those milled from brass, are exquisite pieces of equipment.

Like everything, quality is a very personal thing. Some people I fish with measure quality by how much they pay for an item; others by how well known it is (name); still others, myself included, by performance. I have a couple of reels which I use in salt water that were several hundred dollars each. They are excellent performers for the work I expect. My trout reels, and I own a bunch, were all inexpensive . . . under $50. They too are excellent for what I want and I have used several for over twenty-five years!

Weight of the reel, unless exceptionally light or heavy should not be of much concern. Generally speaking if the reel you choose is "full" (within ¼ inch of the lip of the spool), with 50 to 100 yards of backing plus an entire flyline of whatever line weight your rod handles, then your outfit should balance. That is determined while casting, and with proper balance, reel weight won't be noticed.

21

Although some fly fishers disagree, a good smooth drag system is one of the most important considerations. Big fish don't come along all that often and most are lost because of improper play. Virtually all of us enjoy the direct contact of playing a fish by stripping line by hand. As the fish runs we allow line to slip out through our fingers, applying pressure or releasing depending on the activity of the fish and strength of leader. In essence, our "hand" becomes the drag system.

But big fish will usually take out all the loose line and often even strip backing off the reel. At that point we are playing the fish from the reel and several things become important . . . experience, forgiveness of the rod, leader tippet strength, and drag system.

Assuming you have a single action reel it will be either direct drive or have an anti–reverse drag system. Direct drive means when the handle is turned line is reeled onto the spool; when line is pulled out, the spool and handle spin in direct ratio to line speed. With really big fish like salmon, steelhead, and some Kamloops, a bashed knuckle can result from trying to grab a wildly spinning handle. With monster salt water species like sailfish or tarpon I have even seen broken fingers! Which is why my big reels all have anti–reverse drag systems. These slip–clutch reels allow line to be stripped out while the handle remains stationary. But unless you expect to get into this class of fishing, direct–drive reels will be all you need.

Even then you have choices of drag systems . . . In fact, far too many for us to discuss completely. Probably the best advice is to choose a reel with a simple drag system like a pawl–click setup where pressure is constant and unadjustable. The angle of the pawl allows you to reel in with softer clicks than when line is taken out. The main purpose of this system is to prevent backlash from an overrunning spool. It is very efficient. Another simple system, which allows for some line tension adjustment involves a wing nut or lever on the reel shaft that when tightened puts pressure directly on the spool, both reeling in and going out. It takes a bit of getting used to but is effective. A third system looks like a single brake shoe that pushes against a disk fitted over the reel shaft and attached to the flat side surface of the reel. The disk has a series of angled grooves on its flat side and a spring loaded pin on the spool allows you to reel in with soft clicks and no pressure, yet the pin jams against the straight side of the disk groove when line goes out. The disk then turns and pressure from the brake against the round part of the disk creates tension. It sounds complicated but it's really very simple.

There are several other drag systems, mostly on bigger reels, that are quite complicated. And in the opposite extreme there are also reels with exposed spool rims made for "palming" . . . which means the flat of your hand provides the smoke when the fish heads out.

One other thought . . . Better reels usually have counter balances across from the handle to prevent gyration during a swift run. That is not a problem in our trout lakes, but certainly could be if a single handle reel were used for steelhead or salmon in rivers.

In the final analysis, choose the best quality reel you can based on experience — either your own or those who do a lot of fishing. Like rods, reels also become aesthetic things. Many of us like the feeling of having a balanced outfit with a beautiful rod and matching reel. Anything else might have the appearance of a silk suit with running shoes.

Leaders

The main purpose of a leader is to form a smooth continuation from the tapered fly line on down to the fly. It is also supposed to "hide" the fact that the fly is connected to something . . . a job usually accomplished with good results *if* the fly fisher matches leader tippet to size of the fly being used (more on this later).

A good leader will "unroll" at the end of the cast. This is the culmination of our efforts to balance rod, reel, line and leader . . . so that when we cast, the tapered fly line unrolls easily down through the tapered leader and the fly extends out to the very end of the cast and settles easily onto the water. A fly too heavy for the leader may collapse and drop before it unfolds. And a bushy fly may hold up in the air and then "puddle" down to the water. Both of those situations are usually overcome by using a properly tapered leader with the right stiffness and length to match the fly.

Actual stiffness of the leader material plays a big part in how the fly is presented. Limp leaders usually won't unfold smoothly except with very small flies, and a very stiff leader may uncoil like a spring, slapping the fly down then drawing back. Stiff leaders are prone to holding a set, especially just after coming off the reel. Heating the leader with friction using a pantleg or a special tool of leather and rubber drawn quickly along the leader, then stretching and holding it until it is straight, will usually remove the coils. This is a very important preparation especially for nymph fishing. A fish can mouth your fly and reject it after swimming only a few inches. If your leader is nice and straight you'll see the twitch in your line as the fish moves with the fly; if your leader has coils the fish might swim a fair distance before the leader straightens out enough to move the line.

Length of leader also has a bearing on presentation. I have friends who routinely fish with 20 foot and longer leaders without any problems . . . casting easily and with good distance. My friend Hal Janssen from California, who had had more to do with long leader popularity over the last twenty years than anyone I know, has spent hours coaching me, but I still haven't mastered proper techniques. Believe me, long leaders are tough.

Long leader nymphing is done with a floating line and weighted nymphs. Depending on length of leader, depths to 25 or 30 ft. can be probed. It requires infinite patience as considerable time can elapse between casts.

Recently a "new" system was rediscovered using strike indicators of greased polypro yarn, corks, pieces of floating line slipped over leaders, etc. These indicators (actually bobbers) can be adjusted along the leader to allow flies to hang down below at any depth. They are especially useful on moving waters, but have also gained wide acceptance on lakes. For now I am sticking to more conventional systems . . . but I must admit long leader fishing *does* have its moments!

Like many fly fishers I have spent hours anguishing over conventional leader systems which did not work for me. I suppose in the thirty years I have fly fished and sort-of fly fished, many hundreds of leaders have found their way into my waste bins. I have tried absolutely everything anyone had the patience to show me or I read about. Sometimes they worked, but usually only so-so.

Finally, in a more logical frame of mind, I decided to find one leader system which was at the top side of so-so, and stick with it! Rather than tie my own knotted leaders, which I detest doing, I decided to concentrate on the best quality knotless tapered leaders. My current choices are Aeon and

Berkley. Both are readily available. "My" systems are as follows:

For Use With Floating Lines (I use *only* WF lines) — **Butt Sections:**

WF ⁴/₅ and ⁵/₆ — two feet of 20 lb./stiff monofilament attached to line

WF ⁶/₇ — two feet of 25 lb./stiff monofilament attached to line

WF ⁸/₉ and over — two feet of 30 lb./stiff monofilament attached to line

To these butt sections I add a 9 ft. or 12 ft. tapered leader of 6 lb. test or 4 lb. tip, depending on rod weight and sizes of flies. I can then add a couple feet of 4 lb. tippet or even 2 lb. for small nymphs. With really big patterns like Maribou leeches, Tom Thumbs or dragonfly nymphs, I go to shorter 7½ ft. or 9 foot leaders which are easier to cast as they turn over without collapsing.

Since ninety percent of our B.C. fishing is on lakes or large fast moving rivers like the Thompson, don't worry about being dainty as presentation is not as crucial as on spring creeks when using tiny #20 size flies.

For Use With Sinking Tips (again, I use only WF lines):

Same butt sections, but I use Berkley 7½ foot sinking leaders. They are dulled and have a chemical coating which helps break water surface tension and allows them to sink quickly . . .

For Use With Full Sink Lines

Double Taper — DT I, II — No butt section. I use a 9 ft. Berkley Quick–Sink leader tied directly to the line. It rolls out beautifully.

Weight Forward O, I, II, III — One foot of stiff butt section, same weights as for dry lines, and 7½ foot, sometimes 6 foot, Quick–Sink leaders, tapered to six pound. With full sinking lines shorter leaders are no disadvantage. Under the surface, fish probably see leaders though not like on the surface. Perhaps they even see lines, but I don't believe it really bothers them. I have spent many pleasant hours in my belly boat peering down into the water watching fish approach my fly. *Many* times I have seen fish bump the leader, even "felt" them through the sensitivity of graphite. The real key is how well you are presenting your nymph, not whether the fish see your line.

So leaders are no longer a problem for me, I'm happy to say. If you have the same frustrations give my system a try. I call it "my" system, but certainly it's used by many flyfishers who discovered it long before I was around. I use it because I really don't like tying on leaders all the time. The butt section stays on permanently and I can easily change the tapered leader as it wears down. It's simple, easy and it works for me.

The final point regarding leaders concerns tippets . . . "Tippet" is the lightest test end or tip of a tapered leader. Many flyfishers use knotless tapered leaders as they come out of the package. For instance if a 12 ft. leader is rated 4 lb. test at the tippet, then it can certainly be used as is. After a half-dozen fly changes or break–offs, however, you will be up to about 6 or 7 lb. tippet and your leader will be shorter by a foot or two. At this point we can tie on a two or three foot piece of 4 lb. regular monofilament and again create a 4 lb. tippet. I carry spools of tippet material from 2 lb. test to 10 lb. test, and depending on fly size, use them all, often.

Something many fly fishers, even experienced ones, don't think enough about is the relationship between size of fly and size of leader. It becomes obvious if you have on 8 or 10 lb. tippet material and want to use a small #14 fly . . . the leader won't go through the hook eye. The opposite holds true if you have on 2 lb. tippet and want to use a big #4 leech pattern . . . the first cast or strike and the fly pops the leader. It is important to understand what leader to use: "Generally", 2 lb. is best used with hooks size 10 and smaller; 4 lb. can be used on size 6 down to size 14; 6 lb. on size 2 down to about 10. As you increase leader strength above 6 lb. you will also have to use larger size hooks: for example, 8 lb. test is really too heavy for size 12 hooks, but all right for size 10, 8, and up. Ten pound test leader is too big for size 10 hooks, but okay on size 8 and larger hooks. And so on. This doesn't mean the leader "won't" fit the hole in the hook eye, or that large hooks "can't" be cast with lighter leader tippet. But we get into the realm of making flies appear as natural food (remember, fish have lots of time to observe their food in a stillwater environment . . .!), and there is just no way a little #14 chironomid nymph is going to appear natural when it is hanging stiffly from 8 lb. test leader.

Today's leader materials are becoming much stronger with finer diameters, and in fact are no longer being categorized by weight. Leader tippets are becoming known by diameters: ".006 diameter" instead of 4 lb. test, and ".008 diameter" instead of 6 lb. test, and certainly the smaller the diameter for a given strength, the better for us.

Another classification is the "X" system of grading leader tippet strength where 0X is heavy, usually about 8 lb.,

4X is about 4 or 5 lb., and 7X is down around 1½ lb. . . . depending on the company producing it. There is no real conformity in this system either.

In the final analysis, when you really get into fly fishing, there is still a lot to be learned just about leader systems. If you really want to maximize your dimensions, by all means learn to tie up your own leaders . . . virtually all the well known flyfishers do. In fact some very sophisticated formulas have been created and published, right down to exact inches of material to use, brand names of materials, and specific knots. As mentioned earlier, building leaders is not my thing, but with so many of the best fly fishing people doing it, there must be something to it. Several companies produce leader kits which give instructions and all necessary materials for producing dozens of leaders for varying situations. If nothing else it will give you more knowledge about an extremely gratifying sport.

These few pages barely touch the subject of equipment, but obviously we couldn't get too detailed in such a short space. I hope what we have offered here and on the following pages will provide some insight into the world of fly fishing and encourage you to enjoy its pleasures more.

Knots

Attaching fly to leader

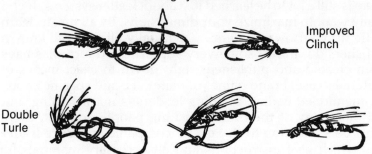

Improved Clinch

Double Turle

Blood Knot
Attaching two leaders together

Nail Knot
Attaching backing and leader to fly line

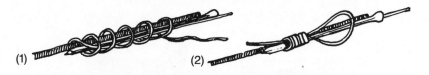

(1)

(2)

(1) Wrap mono around fly line, nail and both lines ·
(2) Put end through coils and tighten

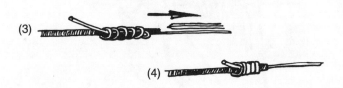

(3)

(4)

(3) Remove nail and slowly tighten
(4) Trim ends

III
Flycasting — Getting the Line Out

by Denise Maxwell

Flycasting is the art of placing an artificial fly in front of a fish so as to imitate its natural food. The fly is carried out by the fly line which is driven by a flyrod.

Fortunately, basic casting is very easy to learn and anyone will be able to go fishing and catch fish after just a few minutes practice. The additional skills needed for more advanced casting can be learned later as your interest in flyfishing grows. Try and go to some organized casting clinics put on by competent flyfishers.

Many a well–intentioned friend has passed on bad casting habits to a beginner.

It is not necessary to have expensive equipment to start flyfishing. There are many inexpensive rod, reel and line outfits suitable for beginners. However, make sure that the rod is matched to cast the numbered line weight. The line must have a tapered leader, and a piece of bright colored wool should be used for the "fly". Eyeglasses or sunglasses should always be worn.

Water is not needed to learn or practice casting and because grass is more available, it is possible to become a proficient caster in the "privacy of your own back yard."

Flycasting consists of a number of movements, each with its own descriptive name, and all are simple to learn. The following lessons should be taken "one step at a time" and practiced regularly for short periods.

Lesson (1) Hand, Arm and Body Position

Strip out ten yards of line, measured from the reel and lay it out in a straight line from the rod tip. Stand facing the direction of the cast with feet apart. Hold the rod with the thumb on top of the cork grip and with the reel on the bottom. Take hold of the line close to the first guide, pull the line down, place your thumb in your pants pocket and keep the line there during practice. Place the butt end of the rod in the sleeve of your shirt or jacket or use a large elastic band to prevent any movement of the wrist during casting. This usually comes as a surprise to people who have been led to believe that it is "all in the wrist". This locked wrist action is vital in learning to cast and most beginners will need a wrist restraining device. See diagram. (1)

Diagram
(1)

Wrist Restraining Device

Lesson (2) Pick Up, Backcast, Forward Cast, Laydown
Consider diagram (2)

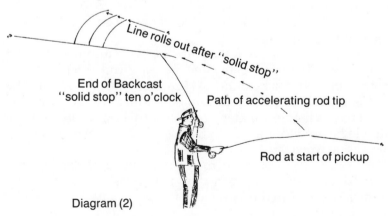

Line rolls out after "solid stop"

End of Backcast
"solid stop" ten o'clock

Path of accelerating rod tip

Rod at start of pickup

Diagram (2)

The caster has picked up the line and driven it upwards and backwards. This has been accomplished by raising the rod tip up at a steady increase in speed and suddenly stopping at about the ten o'clock position with the rod hand at eye height. The arm should be close to the body, grip should be light and the acceleration of the rod tip should be smooth. This causes the line to travel at high speed and to continue on when the stop occurs. There is no need for a "wrist snap" or power stroke at the end of the cast providing the rod tip has been "accelerated correctly" and the wrist has been kept locked.

After the backcast is completed, a slight tug should be felt on the rod tip and this signals the start of the forward cast. The caster now drives the rod tip forward in a straight line towards the fly target with a light and smooth acceleration, stopping at about one o'clock. This movement will cause the line to travel at a high speed and to continue when the sudden stop occurs. Once again, no wrist snap, no wrist rotation (smooth forward motion with steady acceleration). As the line straightens out, the rod tip is lowered at the same rate as the fly and the laydown is complete. Avoid the temptation of giving the line an extra "shot" on the laydown as this action usually tangles the fly and leader. See diagram (3)

Forward Cast and Laydown

Path of accelerating rod tip

Line at end of backcast

line rolls out after "solid stop"

Ten o'clock

End of cast one o'clock "solid stop"

Rod at end of laydown

Diagram (3)

Providing the correct equipment is used and the instructions are followed, adequate casting to fish up to fifteen yards away is possible after only a few minutes of practice.

Lesson (3) False Casting

Sometimes it is necessary to keep the line in the air by casting backwards and forwards. This is called false casting and is used for drying flies, changing the casting direction, and extending line.

False casting is very good for practicing and teaches timing better than any other method. Avoid excessive false casting when fishing as it is seldom necessary. Diagram (4)

False Casting

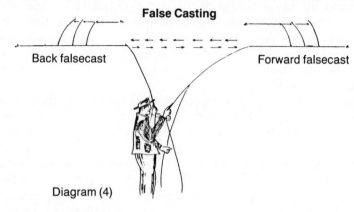

Back falsecast

Forward falsecast

Diagram (4)

Important reminders:
(1) Use matching equipment.
(2) Avoid trying to cast too much line.
(3) Avoid excessive power.
(4) Avoid wrist movement.
(5) Avoid any wrist snap.
(6) Accelerate the rod tip smoothly.
(7) Stop the rod solidly.
(8) Stop the rod at the correct clock position.
(9) Drive the line outwards, not downwards.

In conclusion, it should be noted that this chapter is about basic beginners casting, which should allow fishing up to fifteen yards. However, as the majority of all fish are caught within this range, you are "in business" once you become reasonably efficient.

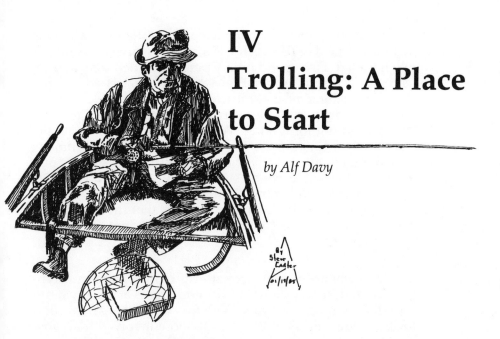

IV
Trolling: A Place to Start

by Alf Davy

As a future fly fisherman, the way you are likely to start to fish with a fly is by trolling it. You probably will have had some experience using gang trolls or flat fish on heavy rods. Now you want to try the mystique of the fly fisher. So you can simply tie a fly on the line and drag it around the lake.

There are times when it is logical even for fly fishermen to troll. It is necessary when you are new to a lake, searching for fish, or if you have non-casters along who can easily get in the way or become bored watching you cast. Also, moving around allows you to study the lake and the insects that drift by the boat.

Equipment

For proper fly fishing have a good net, a couple of anchors and a carpet for the bottom of the boat to eliminate as much noise as possible and to stop you from ruining your expensive fly line when you step on it. You will need a single action reel with thirty meters of backing.

Perhaps it is best to state at the start that you can troll with a fly rod but you cannot fly cast with a trolling rod. You can also troll admirably with an inexpensive fly rod but you may not be able to cast well with it. The good casters you see on the water usually have good equipment. You can troll with monofilament line or any of the fly line types. However, if you want to cast with your trolling outfit you will need to have it equipped with a proper fly line.

33

For trolling there is only one line to start with — a sinking fly line of type II or III which will sink from three to six metres when trolled. Fish spend ninety percent of their time in lakes feeding on insects under the water and that is where you should be fishing most of the time.

Most commercial flies carried in stores are designed for trolling and not for casting. When buying your flies, do not buy them for their looks. The area you fish and the time of year should guide your fly choice. If you are just starting out, ask a good sporting goods store operator in the area which flies are best locally, or buy them at a local fishing lodge. One of the problems with commercial flies is that they tend to be overdressed. So don't buy a big fancy fly just to get your money's worth.

Flies

You will need about six patterns of flies, with each type present in different sizes and colours.That's at least twenty-four different combinations. With four or five of each to allow for loss, you can see this is a little more involved than your standard worm. Which six patterns? I will start with some time–proven flies which will be adequate in all but the most special cases.

Werner Shrimp

The first pattern to buy is a shrimp pattern. There are some good commercial patterns like the Werner Shrimp, Little Guy, and Trueblood Otter. You will need sizes eight to twelve in medium and dark green.

Trueblood

My second purchase would be a Doc Spratley. This is the most famous of the trolling flies. It probably does not represent any one insect but it imitates a leech or a dragonfly (in sizes four to eight), a damsel or caddisfly (in eight or ten) or a chironomid (on twelve or fourteen if you cut most of the hackle off). Black or dark green bodies are the best, but red will work also and they come with a silver or gold ribbing.

Spratley

Trimmed Down Spratley

The third pattern to have would be a Half–Back in sizes eight to twelve to represent smaller natural nymphs of the previous mentioned orders. Other gems are the nymphs such as a Fifty–Two Buick or Idaho Nymph in eight and tens, an attractor like the Black O'Lindsay in eight, ten and twelve and lastly, a floating pattern like a Tom Thumb in sizes eight to twelve which will work for most surface feeding.

34

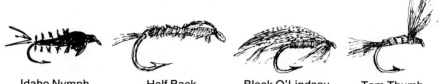

Idaho Nymph   Half Back   Black O'Lindsay   Tom Thumb

As you can see from this list, you would already have a whole box of flies which would still not include specialty ones like the Carey Special, Mosquito, Woolly Worm, Muddler and a hundred others. However, it is best to have a relatively few good patterns rather than so many you get confused and don't know what to use first.

Carey

Woolly Worm

Selection of Flies

What ones do you use first? Try them in the sequence I have listed, starting with the Shrimp and working your way through the Spratley and Half-Back nymph. If they don't work, you try an attractor and start to hope.

How do you know what fly to use? When asking other anglers for information on what fly they are using, start with the colour, then the size. You can ask the name but they may not know, or they may tie their own flies and have their own names. People might tell you the wrong name but very few the wrong colour. If you get the right colour and hook size you have narrowed the possibilities to four or five choices in your box.

At the lake you put your rod, reel, and line together. Your leader should be about the length of your rod to a maximum of about three meters for most people. It should be 3× to 1× (six to eight pounds) in strength. It is best attached to your fly by an improved cinch knot.

Cinch Knot

Where To Start

Ask lodge people or other anglers where they caught fish or saw fish caught or moving. Once on the lake keep a sharp lookout for moving fish, what insects are moving, or where other boats may be catching fish.

Troll around the lake along the drop-off (where shallow and deep water meet) in three to six meters of water. You should be touching bottom with your fly once in awhile to be trolling correctly.

When you do not know a lake, you may have to troll around and look for signs that might help you discover where the fish are. It is always best to fish around islands or shallows in three to six meters of water between or around shoal (aquatic vegetation) areas. As a general rule, do not troll over deep water unless there is fish activity in the area.

Trolling Speed

How fast should you troll? Again, the first rule would be to watch others who might be catching fish and judge their speed. A motor will give a constant speed and rowing will impart to the fly a jerky movement that is more natural and will work better in most cases.

The fact that there is no one correct speed at which you should troll can be illustrated by the following stories. I fished Salmon Lake in the Douglas Lake country one early summer day with my family. My girls were three and five at the time, and as we trolled they held the rods. I was trolling quickly and I could hear comments from other boats that I would never catch anything at that speed. But I had fished the lake the previous weekend and found the fish liked the faster moving fly. We were into fish constantly that day while most others were not.

Some years later, during the same time of year on Sheridan Lake in the Cariboo area of B.C. I was doing very poorly casting a fly. A few old timers were trolling around me and catching fish. I thought I would try to imitate their actions and see if I could have better success with my flies. Their method of "trolling" was to run their boat up the lake against the wind, and then wind drift back down the lake. They would use the oars to hold the boat straight and let the breeze do the rest. It proved to be a very successful way to fish.

There is no secret trolling speed. I have a rule that before I will change flies I always try slow, medium, fast or a combination of speeds, even zig-zags. Often after I have been trolling a fly around at one speed and decide to check the fly for weeds or whatever, after a couple of quick strips of line I get a strike.

Length and Depth of Line

With how much line and what depth do you fish? Again you can watch to see if others are catching fish and determine what they are doing. I usually fish as close to the bottom as I can without getting snagged too often. You want to feel the odd tug now and then. I also like to let out most of my fly line. To make this task easier, learn to strip it in and have it in neat coils on the carpet at your feet. On some lakes, let out half again as much backing as the length of the fly line.

Trolling a fly can also be done without a regular "flyline". I have seen monofilament lines used for trolling both wet and dry flies. You can never get the fly very deep without weights on the line. At times it can be very effective to troll a fly just under the surface very slowly. A deer hair dry fly like the Tom Thumb, Muddler, or D'Mouse can be trolled on the surface with monofilament or a dry fly line. You can troll a chironomid but this method is usually effective when very slowly drifting with the wind. Read the chapter on chironomids and if you cannot cast, try to drift them. You will want as little forward movement as possible, so only row enough to keep the line and boat straight and in contact; that is, so that the line maintains a straight line behind the boat.

Striking

How hard do you strike when a fish bites while trolling? In earlier years of fly fishing when I trolled alone in the boat I often would have two rods out. One I would hold in my hand and the other over my shoulder or between my legs. I used to keep track of which rod did better, and on many days I hooked more fish on the rod I was *not* holding because I did not pull the fly away from an interested fish when it nibbled or struck at the fly. You want to strike only hard enough to make sure the hook will stick in the mouth of the fish. Usually the movement of the boat will do that for you.

Playing A Fish

The successful playing of a fish is easier from a trolled line than a cast line. The reason for this is that a fish is hooked further away from the boat and it's difficult for the fish to get slack line when it jumps if it is pulling against a lot of resistance. When the fish is on, keep the rod tip up and let the rod absorb as much of the shock of the running and jumping as possible. Keep firm but gentle contact with the fish to give and take line as necessary. Most fish are lost close to the boat because there is less resistance for the fish to pull against and the hook will more likely be working its way out. You are now trying to keep calm in order to net the fish and not tangle the line.

Do not hesitate to release fish and only keep what is needed unless the fish is badly hooked or bleeding or the regulations require release. You will undoubtedly get a greater joy from releasing a nice fish than from killing it. If you release the fish, it can grow in size — both as it matures and as you re-tell the tale. If you do kill a fish, do not drag it around in the water. You would not put an expensive beef steak in the water all day and then cook it. Keep it in a cool damp place; a well ventilated container with a wet cloth does nicely. Clean the fish as soon as possible.

Etiquette

When you are trolling on a lake, never troll between a fly caster and the shore area he is working. Do not cut close behind a boat which has lines out. It could have thirty to sixty meters (one hundred to two hundred feet) of line out. Never throw your garbage or fish entrails out of the boat in the lake or on the shore. Take these things home with you so you do not spoil the natural beauty of the lakes. It is up to each of us to see that the fishing environment will remain so that others may enjoy it fully.

By
Steve
Carter
01/19/85

V
Shrimp — The Underwater Clown

by Doug Porter

It was a bright, cool morning and I was anchored alone near a sharp drop–off, patiently dredging the marl bottom 5 meters below with a medium sinking line and a half–back pattern. Two fruitless hours of this casting and retrieving practice were making my mind and vision wander over the surface of the calm lake, searching for any sign of fish. As I turned to observe the courtship ritual of a pair of grebes in the shallows, my gaze caught subtle rings far in the distance. My first reaction was to discount the dimpling I was seeing as ducks feeding. My limited experience fishing for trout in clear water lakes had so far indicated to me that they avoided the shallows, especially during the daylight hours. I thought I might as well row in and have a look. After all, the sun was still below its zenith and the unrippled, clear water would give me an opportunity to view any insect activity.

Keeping the area under surveillance, I slowly rowed backward through the narrow bay toward the mysterious surface disturbance I had seen. Occasional dark patches of weed broke the pattern of the otherwise continuous pale–green marl bottom. I could now see fish but there were no signs of insect activity, so what were they feeding on? My best guess was some small chironomid, since that was the only insect I could think of that would be hatching at this 1100 meter elevation in mid–May.

Anchoring 15 meters west of the activity to keep the shadow of casting and the boat from alarming them, I switched to a dry line with a long leader, knowing fish would be spooked by the heavy slap of a sinking line on the water and by the line itself as it sank among them (at least I'd learned that much during my youthful stream fishing days.)

Tying on a #12 black and white chironomid, I cast, anxiously awaiting the first strike. Time passed slowly as I varied retrieve speeds and depths. Not a touch. I changed to a dark green #12 chironomid and was immediately rewarded with 1 kg. of dancing silver at the end of my line. ''They must be feeding on green chironomids'', I reasoned, as I carefully played the fish to the net. A quick blow to the head dispatched the fish so the stomach contents could be examined. (In those early days, I killed the fish to determine what they were feeding on). Now I use a stainless steel probe which, when inserted down the throat, extract samples of the latest organisms on which the fish has been feeding, allowing it to be released unharmed after this 3 to 5 second procedure.) I was surprised to find that the fish had been feeding exclusively on immature Gammarus shrimp which were pale to dark green in colour and approximately 1 cm. long. The rest of the morning went quickly as I caught and released several more fish up to 1.5 kg. after switching to a #12 medium green Werner Shrimp and a slow sinking line. This change was made so the fly could be fished close to the bottom where the fish were feeding.

Gammarus shrimp

Shrimp

Reflecting back to this incident, which occurred early in my fly fishing development, I realized that a number of beliefs to which I had doggedly clung had been erroneous and in fact:

1) That during certain conditions, trout will move into shallow water to feed during daylight hours in clear water (I had already learned that they would feed among the lily pads during the day in darker or acidic waters).

2) The dimpling I had observed were trout taking the occasional shrimp which was moving just under the surface. It didn't indicate an insect hatch!

3) That by using a long leader, and a gentle cast, I could deliver the fly just beyond the fish without spooking them.

4) That when it comes to fish behaviour, nothing can be taken for granted and that trout are where you find them.

In the 60's, fly fishing was a trial and error sport, with very little literature about local techniques, methodology or entomology available to the layman. I began at that time, however, to acquire every article and book written about the subjects that I could find. Subsequently, combined with many hours of experience and observation, I have learned a great deal about the two genera of shrimp (scud) most likely to be encountered in B.C. lakes.

Gammarus shrimp or scuds can be found in any unpolluted hard water lake, living close to the bottom in depths up to 20 meters, preferring however, the shallower waters up to 4 meters deep. Their size can reach lengths up to 2.5 cm. and they can be many different colors which is a product of their environment and food source. This consists of microscopic plant and animal matter which has settled to the bottom. The Gammarus swims short distances of 15–30 cm., then rests in a curled position as it slowly settles downward. It is primarily a nocturnal feeder, hiding under rocks, logs, in the weeds, or in the marl bottom during daylight hours, except during mating which occurs several times during the year.

Hyalella is another scud which is very similar to Gammarus except it is much smaller (rarely exceeds 0.75 cm. in length) and can be found in more acidic environments. Perhaps a good rule of thumb for determining acidity or alkalinity of Interior lake water is by its clarity. Acidic water is usually darker in colour, often contains lily pads which prefer the more acidic waters and it is difficult to see the bottom in depths over 1–2 meters.

Where Gammarus shrimp are found in abundance, they provide the main diet and account for the rapid growth and fighting qualities characteristic of the Kamloops trout. Shrimp will only be ignored during major emergencies or migrations of other insects, or when warm water temperature limits feeding forays into shallower waters.

Scud

Care must be taken then, where shrimp are the primary source of food, to ensure that overstocking of fish does not occur, which could seriously deplete the shrimp population and possibly result in reduced or stunted fish growth. Not only is growth rate seriously affected, but the health and table quality of the fish could suffer as well.

Under most conditions I have found it is best to use a slow to medium sinking line with at least a 4 m. leader length tapering to a 2 kg. or lighter tippet. This method keeps the fly close to the bottom. Slow pulls of 15-30 cm. should be used with 2-5 second pauses to imitate the resting periods. Identification of the size and colour of the shrimp to be imitated is crucial. The colour of the fly should match the habitat over which it is fished. Early morning and later afternoon when light levels are low usually find the shrimp more active, but there are always numerous variables which can influence the activities of both the shrimp and the trout.

Over the years I have blended various colours of wool and seal fur to match the bottom colour, whether it be weeds or marl and I have found, through experimentation, that a fly which is two tone in colour with a darker shade over the back and lighter underneath with a sparse hackle produces best. (Doug's Drifter)

A number of commercial patterns will also fool trout if fished properly. They are the Werner shrimp, Baggie shrimp, Dexheimer sedge, Green Carey, and Black O'Lindsay in sizes 8 to 14.

Black O'Lindsay   Shrimp   Carey

Gammarus.

Fishfood Profile
Common Name: *Gammarus* Shrimp (Scud)
Taxonomic Classification: Class Crustacea, Order Amphipoda
Size Range: 10-25 mm. in length
Colouration: Various shades of yellow, brown, green and grey dependent on habitat conditions
Preferred Habitat: *Gammarus* are typically found within the first 7 metres of depth where they seek refuge in vegetation, rocky areas or debris piles. They are omnivorous

scavengers feeding on both plant and animal matter. The distribution of *Gammarus* is restricted to waters having higher levels of calcium and total dissolved solids which are required for formation and maintenance of the exoskeleton. Dark water, lily pad lakes would not be a preferred habitat of this shrimp species.

Scuds.

Availability to Trout: Where available, *Gammarus* are a staple component of the diet of trout.

Life Cycle: These shrimp are prolific breeders producing up to 7 broods per year. Mating shrimp are identified by the "piggyback" position frequently observed as the female rides the male's back. Pregnant females are identified by an orange–red brood pouch located on the underside of the body.

Distinguising Features: *Gammarus* attain much larger sizes than *Hyalella* shrimp but are more restricted in their distribution due to water chemistry requirements.

Fishfood Profile
Common Name: *Hyalella* Shrimp
Taxonomic Classification: Order Amphipoda, Class Crustacea
Size Range: 2–8 mm. in length
Colouration: lighter shades of yellow, green and blue dependent on habitat occupied.

Preferred Habitat: *Hyalella* are capable of living in a wide variety of lake types including both acidic and alkaline conditions. They are omnivorous scavengers feeding on zooplankton, detritus and animal matter. These shrimp are commonly found in depths of less than 7 metres as they seek refuge in vegetation mats or marl areas.

Availability to Trout: Year round, although possibly more available as the water temperatures increase and the shrimp are more active.

Life Cycle: Females are capable of breeding or producing offspring numerous times per year. Mating shrimp are those observed riding "piggyback" through the water.

Distinguishing Features: *Hyalella* sp. are much smaller in size

43

than the *Gammarus* shrimp and often their colouration is paler. They also tolerate much wider water chemistry conditions such as lower pH lakes.

VI.
A. Chironomidae: The Slow Motion Wiggler

by Jim Crawford

Probably the most important aspect of fishing is learning about the various aquatic invertebrates that trout feed on! Without that knowledge even the most sophisticated caster will be severely limited. Fortunately, the characteristics of aquatic invertebrates in our B.C. fresh water environments is fairly easy to study: each major species has unique patterns of movement and behaviour that once learned, will be easily recognized wherever you fish.

In their "common name" aquatic forms, dragonflies, damselflies, chironomids, mayflies, stoneflies, sedges, water beetles, leeches, shrimp, and (to a small degree) snails, make up the major trout foods in our B.C. Interior waters. Different species can be more or less dominant depending on environmental factors within each body of water. All of these are important to the flyfisher and methods of imitating particular behavioral characteristics of most are described in this book by fishermen who are especially knowledgeable about that particular group.

Of all the major fish foods mentioned, only one group can be expected in virtually every aquatic habitat, and in lakes will nearly always be dominant simply by their sheer numbers. This group is the order Diptera or true flies which are better known as midges. To the average person, "midge" describes a multitude of tiny insects, including mosquitoes, black-flies, no-see-ums and so-called "buzzers". To the flyfisher, "midge" refers to the chironomidae which are unquestionably the most important source of insect feed for stillwater trout of all sizes. It's hard to believe, but these tiny creatures, many only ¹/₁₆ to ¹/₄ inch in length and about as thick as a pencil lead, sustain trout of every size. While many flyfishers search for better known hatches of mayflies or sedges, the knowledgeable flyfisher concentrates on chironomids . . .

It wasn't too many years ago that only a handful of flyfishers knew anything at all about chironomids. In the 40's, "mosquito" nymphs and "sand fly" nymphs were being tied in the western U.S., and in the 50's "midge" nymphs made an appearance there. However, it wasn't until the early 1960's that patterns tied specifically to represent "chironomids" were popularized in British Columbia. Undoubtedly there were many flyfishers over the years who recognized the importance of chironomids and almost certainly some tied representative patterns. But it was Jack Shaw of Kamloops who must be recognized as the true pioneer of B.C. chironomid patterns and methods of using them. Some years later, and quite independently, came the PKCK chironomid patterns created by Dave Powell and Jim Kilburn. Being less secretive about their discoveries, the Powell and Kilburn chironomids quickly became popular and widely used. Today, chironomid nymph patterns of every size and color are in virtually every knowledgeable flyfisher's fly box, and try as some of us might to play down the effectiveness of these patterns, they are definitely here to stay.

Characteristics

Because of their importance to flyfishers, characteristic descriptions of behaviour for this very large family, chironomidae, can be covered in general terms. Size and color are the most obvious differences, and various methods and techniques of using representative patterns, will be covered in this book by two well-known fly fishermen, Tim Tullis of Hatheume Lake Resort, and Alf Davy of Kelowna. Additional detailed information on chironomid fishing can also be learned from the true master, Jack Shaw, in his own book, *Fly Fish the Trout Lakes.*

All chironomidae go through complete metamorphosis in their life cycle of egg, larva, pupa, and winged adult. The term "nymph" is used to describe their aquatic stages of growth ("nymph" also describes subsurface fly patterns used to imitate any of the aquatic invertebrates). As flyfishers we concentrate primarily on the two nymphal stages, larval and pupal. The winged adult is not "usually" an important source of trout food except under special circumstances (such as when very large chironomids are hatching).

Larvae

Chironomid larvae are thin, wormlike creatures with segmented body sections, and vary in length from "very tiny" up to an inch. Virtually all growth takes place during the larval stage, which can last up to two years in cold northern regions, though one year or less is more common. Although some species are free-swimming and some others construct elaborate cases similar to sedges, most chironomid larvae live in mud tubes on the lake bottom and go through several instars or molts before changing into pupae. As larvae go, they are good swimmers and often move in dense numbers to feed, to find new "homes" when increased size forces them out, or to migrate into deeper water to overwinter. Anytime larvae move away from their sanctuary they are easy prey which trout seldom pass up . . . sometimes absolutely gorging themselves. An astute flyfisher will recognize when such feeding occurs, usually in spring and early summer, and again in fall just before ice up.

Patterns should represent the bright red, maroon and red-brown colors of larvae, which reflect hemoglobin (red) showing through thin skin. These are referred to as "bloodworms", and indeed they do take on that character. But I have also seen bright green, yellow, purple, and nearly transparent larvae, so the flyfisher should have a good selection of colours. Sparse, thinly tapered bodies in sizes 18 to 8, with a slight hackle on larger sizes, fished slowly across the bottom and over weeds will do the trick. When . . .? Anytime, but especially in spring and fall when not much is going on at the surface.

Pupae

Characteristics of chironomid pupae are much easier to identify than larvae, and hold the most promise for angling success, even though they are in the pupal stage only a short period of time.

After their final molt as larvae, chironomids seal themselves inside a cocoon-like structure to undergo change into pupae . . . much the same as sedges. Usually within hours (but sometimes as long as a week) after emerging as pupae, chironomids begin their ascent towards the surface in a stop-and-go swimming motion to undergo final emergence as winged adults. Aided by pockets of gas within the thoracic hump, buoyancy as well as built-in upright orientation is provided to help the pupal nymph in its swim towards the

surface which can be two hundred or more feet away . . . though less than forty feet is more usual. As pupae ascend they take periodic rest stops, and fish can lazily pick them off at any point between the bottom and the surface film. Precise pattern imitations become crucial with pupae because trout have the advantage of observing these subsurface forms in a totally quiet, distortion–free environment.

Chironomid hatches in B.C. will occur almost daily from ice–off right through summer, depending on water temperature and sun declination, the two "best" months being May and June. Late morning through late afternoon are often the most productive times. Probably the thing you'll notice most as you sit on your favourite lake watching hordes of adult chironomids take flight, is the variety of sizes and the different body colours. It would be unusual for only one specie to be hatching . . . but not unusual that trout are only taking one kind! You may have to change patterns several times to find the one that fish are feeding on most predominantly. Usually it means capturing nymphs as they wiggle to the surface or spooning a fish's stomach in order to match size and colour of the hatch. Your fly patterns should then show basic body colour set off with contrasting ribbing of white, gold, silver, copper, black, etc. to match segmentation. Predominant colors will be shades of black, gray, brown, green, and amber, and adults will nearly always be brighter than the pupae so if you are using adults as your colour guides, bear that in mind.

Tunkwanamid.   Mosquito Larva.   Small Black.

Chaoboridae

At this point one other group of midge should be mentioned: Chaoborus, the phantom midge. Primarily nocturnal, phantom midges normally inhabit deep–water regions of lakes during daylight hours, either in mud tubes on the bottom or actually suspended in low–light areas over deep zones. When found in low nutrient lakes, chaoborus larvae can move upwards with the aid of specialized air bladders into more productive waters near the surface to feed on micro–organisms at night, and descend back down with daylight. These are the fabled "glass worms" and "mystery midges" which hatch at night or during early morning hours. Trout sometimes feed on the larvae of this insect to the exclusion of all else, and when that happens you might as well go pick mushrooms . . . That is because this species is very difficult to match with fly patterns. It is generally up to ½ inch long, and completely transparent except for two opposing black spots. Clear monofiliment line dyed in weak tea and wrapped around the hook will sometimes be effective, but it's not usually worth the effort. I mention this midge because you can save yourself a lot of frustration by recognizing when trout are on it.

Pupae of this species are usually an off-white or pale yellow and can be matched with more conventional pupal patterns.

One Hint

As mentioned, actual fishing methods are covered elsewhere, but in general, good chironomid techniques will require casting into deep water, over drop-offs, and up onto shoals, so a boat or float tube is an absolute must. A soft rod, floating or sinking lines to fish different depths, and tapered leaders of 6 to 12 feet plus ample tippet material from 2 lb. to 6 lb. test for different hook sizes will start you out.

After more than twenty-five years of stillwater fly fishing, I can safely say bigger fish prefer to feed in bottom regions. There are exceptions, of course, as when big traveller sedges flutter across the surface, or when adult mayflies sit quietly like tiny sailboats. But generally, big fish stay in the bio-productive zones of the bottom. Keep that in mind as you watch a good chironomid hatch and fish are moving all around you at the surface . . . It takes great dedication to probe the bottom in a situation like that.

And now to the fun parts . . .

VI B
Chironomidae: Floating Line Techniques

by Alf Davy

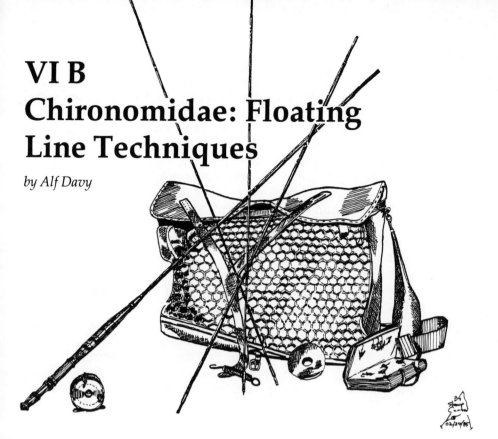

My first introduction to chironomid fishing in lakes with a floating line was from a fishing acquaintance in the Kamloops area. He told me that all I had to do to catch fish on a chironomid pattern was anchor my boat, cast the line out, set the rod across the oars and watch the line. When the line moved I was to strike. It all–seemed too simple to me. But it does describe many of the elements I now use when fishing with chironomids.

Strike Indicator

The simplest way to fish chironomids is to "dead drift" (no movement of line or fly) a dry line and standard unweighted patterns. Use sizes ten and twelve, in black, green, and brown, with a small piece of fluorescent yarn tied to the leader just below the fly line. The yarn, treated with a good floatant, will act as a strike indicator and when adjusted along the leader allows you to fish whatever depth you wish to the maximum length of your leader — usually four or five meters.

The best way to fish from a boat is to anchor it front and rear so the wind will not move it around. Fishing with the wind, cast the line fifteen to twenty meters, then sit quietly and watch the indicator, keeping the line as straight as possible. When a fish takes, the indicator will pop under water or move a few centimeters and you must lift the rod steadily and set the hook.

In bad light or windy conditions use a strike indicator to help you see the end of your fly line. It is also an aid for the novice chironomid flyfisher.

The best size of leader tippet is as light as you can handle without breaking fish off. If you have a nice soft rod you might use three pound test. But with a stiff rod you will need five or six pound. A good rule is to use as long and light a leader as you are capable of handling without having casting problems, wind knots, or leader tangles.

Slow Retrieve

Once you have mastered the dead drift method of fishing the chironomid you might want to remove the indicator and go to the next method of fishing where you retrieve the line very slowly. Wherever possible cast with the wind from a boat anchored over a shoal area. By casting with the wind your "contact" with the fly becomes easier. Again, use a leader about the same length as the depth of the water, to a maximum of 4 or 5 meters.

Flies

I have a selection of weighted chironomids in my fly box for fishing deeper shoal areas of three to seven meters. To weight a fly, add a wrapping of lead fuse wire or the lead from lead core trolling line. Wrap the lead along the shank of the hook before tying in the fly body. There are a couple of ways to tell which flies are weighted. Use a different colour tying thread on these flies or keep all weighted flies in a separate fly box. If you do not tie your own flies then use a split shot to get the fly down.

With this second method of chironomid fishing using weighted or unweighted flies, I use a standard three to four meter leader with a tippet tied on to make whatever leader length is needed. To start I always stretch the leader material to make it as straight as possible so the slightest movement can be seen. A fish can take your fly, move several centimeters and reject it, and you will never know it happened if your leader has coils in it.

Depth

I normally cast out eighteen to twenty-five meters of fly line and then wait until I feel the fly has reached the desired depth. How do you know when the fly is deep enough? One way is to drop it over by the side of the boat and watch it sink, timing or counting how long it takes. When you know the sink rate of the fly then cast and wait the necessary time for it to sink.

The Take

Once the fly is at the desired depth, very slowly start your retrieve. I always point my rod tip down so I can lift the rod rather than wrist–snap on the strike as often happens when the rod is held up. Retrieve the fly inch by inch keeping the line straight and in direct contact with the fly. Concentrate on the strike indicator if you use one, or on the fly line out as far as you can see it. That may be the very end, or under poor conditions, much closer in, and watch for any small movement of the line. It may only twitch a few centimeters or be a slight straightening of a bend in the line, but whatever, when the fish has taken in the fly the hook must be set before it can be expelled. Again, simply lift rod and arm to set the hook rather than snap the rod upwards.

The real key to successful dry line fishing is concentration on the fly line or strike indicator at all times. You will hook a far greater number of fish and break off fewer if you see the movement of the line rather than feel the fish take.

Long Leader and Weighted Flies

A third way to dry line chironomid fish is with very long leaders and weighted patterns. This method is used when fishing deep drop–off areas. The leader will be up to eight meters in length and you must use a weighted pattern or it will take forever to sink. Find a drop–off area where the bottom slopes down from three to ten meters very steeply. Either anchor in the deep area and cast in along the shoal, or anchor up on the shoal and cast out over the drop–off or along the drop–off. Let the weighted fly sink and watch the line very carefully. It is very important that the leader turns over when cast as the fly must sink from a straight leader and not a coiled one or any take on the way down will go unnoticed. Again, the take will almost always be very gentle so concentration on line is essential.

This method of chironomid fishing is a compromise between floating and sinking line fishing where a weighted fly is used to get down deep rather than using the weighted line. The next logical step is to learn sinking line techniques. But beginning chironomid fishermen find it so easy to adapt the floating line methods described here, and, in fact, usually experience such good success, they often never use sinking lines for chironomid fishing.

VI C
Chironomidae: Sinking Line Techniques

by Tim Tullis

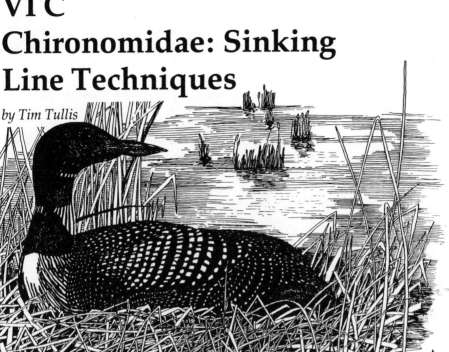

LOON

Over the past ten years or so there has been a great deal written and a lot of discussion about chironomid fishing with the dry or floating line. There is an alternative. It is chironomiding with a sinking line. Don't get me wrong, I enjoy fishing chironomids with a dry line. It is successful and brings back memories of fishing as a kid with a bobber and worm. However the sinking line technique can really be deadly.

My first introduction to wet line chironomid fishing took place on a perfect spring day about nine years ago. An extremely strong chironomid hatch started early in the day and I spent the morning fishing my private little bay using the standard dry line technique with only fair success. A dozen or so fly changes looking for the right size and colour had finally produced a couple of nice fish. I remembered to spoon the second fish before releasing it. The stomach contents told me that I had stumbled on to a chironomid fly pattern that was close to most of the naturals on which the fish were feeding. close to most of the naturals on which the fish were feeding.

But a couple more hours of serious fishing produced only a half dozen fish. This was frustrating. The hatch was strong and armed with the right fly, it should have been a fish a cast. Only two possibilities were left; either there was something wrong with my technique or my favorite little spot was short on fish. After a little thought I opted to pull anchor and look for greener pastures. I soon found a group of a half dozen fisherman working a deep hole on the edge of a large flat area. All were anchored on the edge of the drop off and fishing the deep water. Everyone seemed to be fishing chironomids with a dry line with only moderate success. There was one exception, however, and this fisherman landed and released four fish as I was approaching the group. As I moved closer I recognized Jack Shaw who is virtually a fly fishing legend in the Kamloops area. The lesson was about to start.

I anchored a little to Jack's left, poured a cup of coffee, suppressed the urge to pick up my rod and just sat back to watch Jack fish. It was unbelievable. He hooked a fish on every cast for the hour or so I sat and talked to him. The difference, of course, was that Jack was using a sinking line. On this particular day the sinking line was out-fishing the floating line technique ten to one even though the fish were gorging themselves on chironomids. After talking to Jack the answer became clear. The day was bright causing the fish to stay in deeper water for cover. Jack's sinking fly was getting down to the fish in a matter of a few seconds and was staying there. With the floating line technique, even with a twenty foot leader, the fly would take too long to reach the desired depth and retrieving would cause the fly to rise away from the fish.

The years since that eventful day have given me numerous opportunities to experience the various aspects of wet line chironomid fishing. This technique can be used any time there is chironomid activity but there are times when it is by far the most productive method. As previously described it is extemely successful on bright days when the fish tend to stay in deeper water. It is also the best choice in windy conditions when it becomes difficult to detect a take with a dry line because the line in wind is so hard to see. And, of course, when chironomids are coming from depths in excess of twenty feet, the wet line is always my first choice.

The most important piece of equipment for fishing chironomids with a sinking line is your rod. It must be soft! If your fly pattern is a good imitation of the natural, the take will be extremely light. In fact, as the fish cruises off with your fly you normally will not feel anything until your line and leader tighten up. At the same time the fish will also discover that something is wrong and panic. If the fisherman sets up (strikes) at the same time the fish is in full flight the end result will be a broken leader unless a very soft rod is used to absorb the shock. A good choice of rod would be one 9 feet or longer, rated for a four or five weight line. The longer rod also makes it easier to cast while sitting down in your boat or while fishing from a float tube.

There are a number of basic sinking lines on the market that have special applications. They range from neutral density (extremely slow sinking) to deep water express (sinks like a rock). But for the purpose of chironomid fishing we will consider the three most useful types. They are the Type I or slow sinking line, Type II or fast sinking line and the 10 foot sink tip which can be purchased with nearly any sink rate you desire.

I like to use a slow sinking line when fishing along the edge of drop offs or on flats when the water is 10 to 20 feet deep. A slow sinking line will sink at a rate of approximately 2 inches (5cm.) per second or 10 feet a minute.

The 10 foot sinking tip line will sink quite rapidly to a depth of 8 or 9 feet then slow considerably due to the floating portion of the line. It is my choice when fishing deep depressions in weed beds. It is also very effective when anchored in shallow water fishing over the edge of a drop off.

The Type II sinking line sinks at a rate of 3 or 4 inches (7.5 to 10cm.) a second and is best used when fishing water deeper than 20 feet. Chironomid fishing with a fast sinking line can be very effective during the mid-summer doldrums when the fish have moved into deeper water.

Keeping the speed at which your line sinks in mind, you can count or time your line to any desired depth. But at this point, there is still a bit of a guessing game involved to get your fly to the right level. There are other factors to consider such as the size and weight of your fly, leader diameter and length, speed of your retrieve and amount or height of weed growth on the bottom. My approach to finding the right depth is to count the fly line down to a level I guess will produce success. If I hit weeds or snag the bottom I shorten the sink time on the next cast. If I don't snag bottom or get weeds and don't get a take from a fish, I let the fly sink a little longer on the next cast. Usually 3 or 4 casts will get you to the correct depth.

The question of leaders can lend itself to hours of debate. Rather than going into a long discussion on the merits of various leaders, I will offer what works best for me. I use a short leader about 6 feet when fishing chironomids with a sinking line.

I have a better feel for where my fly is with a short leader and have never found leader length mades any difference to the fish when I am using a sinking line. For leader tippet size, I usually use a 4× going to 5× in very clear water.

The chironomid patterns I like to use are tied on hook sizes 10 to 16 standard, and, at times, on longer shank hooks. I prefer to use thin-bodied patterns in black, brown, dark grey and dark shades of green tied with polycryolin or dubbed rabbit fur. Commercially tied patterns that will work are the TDC nymph, small halfback nymph, small pheasant tail nymph or a stripped down Doc Spratley. Some fly fishing shops now offer their own series of chironomid or midge nymph patterns.

The chironomid nymph is not much of a swimmer. When it comes out of the mud and starts for the surface to hatch it does so in a wiggling motion. It will wiggle and rise a few inches, stop and quietly settle a little, then wiggle and move up again. This routine is repeated over and over and eventually it works its way to the surface. To imitate this movement you can use a short stripping retrieve or an over-hand crawl retrieve (hand twist). The technique is to only move your fly an inch or two at a time and to pause after each movement. The key is to retrieve *slowly*. When you think you have it about right, slow it down a little more. With your fly coming more or less straight up from the bottom keep your eye on your rod tip. The take, remember, will usually be soft . . . only a slight tightening of your line.

Now that you have added chironomid fishing to your fly fishing arsenal, you will improve your fishing success ration tremendously. Try pinching the barb on your fly and remember, every fish you release unharmed today is a fish we all may have a chance to catch tomorrow.

Entomology Profile
Common Name: Chironomids (Midges, Buzzers)
Taxonomic Classification: Order Diptera, Family Chironomidae

Size Range: 2–25mm. in length for all stages of life cycle.
Colouration: Larva — most common colours include shades of yellow, green, brown and red.

Pupa — most prominent are shades of brown, green and black.

Adult — similar to pupa.

Preferred Habitat: Chironomid larvae are bottom dwellers that can live at depths of up to 70 metres. They typically live in tubes constructed within the mud-water interface. Where mud is not the substrate, the larvae will construct living tubes out of sand, vegetation or detritus. The larvae are equipped with a set of prolegs at each end of their slender, wormlike body. Some species are capable of swimming. They achieve this by twisting their body in a creeping fashion. Chironomid larvae are chiefly herbivorous, feeding on vegetation, algae and organic debris. One reason for the very wide distribution and species diversity of Chironomids is their ability to live in oxygen-poor waters. Larvae of these species possess hemoglobin in their circulatory system which, through a biochemical process, releases oxygen for respiration. These larvae are recognized by their deep red colouration and are referred to as "bloodworms".

Availability to Trout: Chironomid larvae are available year round but are probably more active as water temperatures rise. Occasionally during strong winds large masses of larvae (particularly bloodworms) are lifted off the bottom and become easy prey for trout.

It is during the pupal ascent to the surface that Chironomids are most heavily preyed upon. Trout will literally gorge themselves on pupae to the point of almost bursting their stomachs.

As adults, it is the egg-laying females, whether sitting on the water or flying low with just the abdomen touching, that attract the interest of trout.

Lakes that are ice-free all year can experience continual Chironomid hatches. In the Interior of British Columbia where most lakes are frozen over for more than half the year, the most intense hatches occur in May and June.

Life Cycle: Most Chironomid species have a one year generation or life cycle. As the larva develops and grows it may go through as many as six molts. When mature it seals the tube and begins the change into the pupa. This transformation may take up to several weeks dependent on environmental factors such as water temperature. The fully developed pupa is distinguished by a very large thoracic section which contains the wings of the adult. White filamentous tufts are prominant at the head and to a lesser degree at the tip of the

abdomen. Both are used in respiration. The pupa then wiggles out of the old larval tube and begins its ascent to the surface. Their voyage upward is assisted by air trapped beneath the pupal skin. Constant undulating motion of their bodies helps to maintain a position in the water of more or less head up and tail down. The pupa must again exert considerable wriggling motion to break through the surface film. The pupal skin then splits along the back and an adult crawls out onto the surface film. The transformation of the pupa to adult at the surface generally takes less than two minutes.

The adult Chironomid then flies off to mate. Females return to deposit eggs in the surface film. Typical egg laying occurs on calm water preferrably in the morning or late evening. Females can be seen sitting on or flying over the surface film with their abdomens touching the water as they release their eggs. The eggs sink to the bottom of the lake and complete the cycle.

Distinguishing Features: Chironomid larvae are easily recognized by the distinct segmentation of their worm-like body. The prolegs are also visible to the naked eye. ''Bloodworm'' larvae are common in almost all Interior lakes.

Pupae are identified by the tufts of white breathing filaments protruding from the head and, to a lesser degree, from the tip of the abdomen. An enlarged thorax is also noticeable as it encases the fully developed wings. The abdomen is also distinctly segmented.

Adult Chironomids can be distinguished from adult mosquitoes by the fact that the female Chironomid does not bite and when sitting, the mosquito rests with its hind legs in the air. Adult Chironomids can be sexed by the feathery plumose antennae possessed by the male versus the slender shorter ones of the female.

VII
May Flies: Elegance in Stillwater

by Brian Chan

By
Steve
Carter
01/19/8

I arrived at my predetermined fishing spot early so there was ample time to rig my rods up and double check knots, leaders and flies. Conditions were perfect: a slightly overcast day, light breeze and ideal water temperatures. It started with the odd bulging rise as the trout started feeding on emerging nymphs just subsurface. Then the first adults became visible, appearing to almost pop out of the water. Soon, enough duns were on the water that the trout began feeding in earnest. Floating nymphs disappeared in head and tail rises while slashing swirls marked the locations of newly emerged duns. Nighthawks, appearing from nowhere began their swooping dives as they picked off more of the duns. A good fish was methodically feeding within casting range. Staying low so as not to spook the fish, I began working out line and placed a cast where I anticipated his next rise. The dun imitation disappeared in a violent swirl and line began to peel off the reel. This was not fishing a Montana spring creek but an Interior B.C. lake. Contrary to common belief, B.C. offers some excellent mayfly fishing in both coastal and interior still waters.

Mayflies and their Lake Habitat

Almost 600 species of mayflies have been identified as inhabiting the lakes and streams of North America. Less than 10% of these are lake or still water inhabitants. The most common species encountered on interior B.C. lakes are of the *Callibaetis* and *Caenis* genera. The *Callibaetis* or "speckled-winged" species have perhaps the widest distribution and are of most interest to the flyfisher.

The *Caenis* species are very minute in size and not as

widely distributed. To date, there has been only minor attention paid to this mayfly but techniques discussed for *Callibaetis* fishing apply directly to this genus as well.

Callibaetis nymphs and adults range in size from 3 to 12 mm. in length and thus can be imitated well on 14 standard and 12 extra long shank hooks. Most common nymph colouration includes undersides of yellow, olive, or tan and dorsally, darker shades of tan to charcoal grey. The dun and spinner stages have body colouration ranging from dark brown to charcoal grey.

Caenis nymphs and adults are generally 2 to 5 mm. in length excluding tails. Imitations are best represented on hooks from 20 standard to 16 long shank. Nymphs are most often tan or medium brown in colour while dun and spinner forms are almost always creamy white.

Lakes with extensive shallow or shoal areas, in combination with cover such as submergent vegetation, large rocks or woody debris, offer ideal mayfly habitat. When combined with waters rich in calcium and nutrients, you have the typical interior lake and the potential for a good mayfly population.

Within the shoal or shallow zone, the mayfly nymphs feed on detritus and vegetation and utilize available cover for protection from predacious invertebrates as well as foraging fish. These habitat requirements generally limit mayfly nymph distribution to a depth of seven meters.

Emergence Times

In the southern Interior (Williams Lake south), the first *Callibaetis* hatches usually occur by mid–May dependent on ice–off and water temperatures. The most prolific hatches occur from late May to mid–July.

Caenis hatches normally occur from late June to mid–August, again dependent on water temperature. Sporadic hatches of both varieties will occur throughout the summer and fall and will usually trigger activity. Anglers would benefit by keeping track of hatches at their local or favourite lakes since these hatches should occur annually at about the same time.

Generally, overcast skies and cool gentle breezes offer the best conditions for mayfly emergence. These factors allow a prolonged hatch and offer the most predator protection to the emerging nymphs and adults. These periods are also the best times for the flyfisher as shadows, line and boat disturbances are also masked by the light and water conditions.

Actual emergence seems to be most prolific between

10:00 am. and 3:00 pm., though local weather conditions may delay or prolong hatches. Spinner-falls or the return of egg-laying females usually occur in the very early daylight hours or just prior to darkness.

Anglers should also remember that immature mayfly nymphs are active throughout the year and are readily sought after by trout.

Feeding Habits of Trout

Much has been written about this topic particularly as it applies to flowing waters. The prevailing message is that trout can be very selective when feeding on mayflies. When fishing moving waters the challenge is often overcoming tricky current patterns to achieve a "drag-free drift" as the fly is presented to a stationary trout. In lakes, the challenge is different but just as difficult. With no current, the angler must impart realistic movement to the emerging nymph pattern and present it to feeding trout. Similarly, dun and spinner imitations must be realistically imitated as well as properly presented.

Trout often select the immature nymphs which hide among the vegetation or other cover of a shoal area. In this situation, the fish show no visible feeding signs to the angler except under very clear water conditions. The trout cruise among the bottom cover and then suddenly turn around to pick up a nymph caught away from cover.

Maturing nymphs are selected throughout their emergence-swim to the surface. Specifically, the nymphs are taken just as they leave the bottom cover, as they reach the surface and when laying in the surface film just prior to emergence as a dun. Knowing when to fish the proper imitations is based on understanding the mayfly life cycle and fishing at the appropriate time of year.

It is within the top one meter of water that the trout show telltale signs of what stage of nymph they are feeding on. Bulging rises where the trout may show part of its back, generally indicates feeding on emerging nymphs within 10 to 30 cm. of the surface. Head and tail rises often reveal the fish are selecting the nymph just subsurface or in the surface film. Splashy rises signal the presence of newly-emerged duns and the most exciting part of mayfly fishing. The return of egg-laden females or the spinner-fall is generally met by bulging riseforms as the trout almost methodically sip in the spent insects. At other times, the trout will literally "gulp" mouthfuls of spinners.

Equipment Selection and Fishing Strategies

Equipment selected for general lake use is quite adequate

for mayfly fishing. However, because of the often delicate fishing techniques and relatively small imitations used, some anglers prefer to use a light rod in the 3.0 to 3.5 meter length capable of casting lines in the 5 and 6 weight range. The various life stages on which the trout feed requires the use of several types of flylines. These include slow sinking, intermediate sinking, sink–tip and floating lines. Perhaps the floating line is the most important as it can be used for all nymph stages as well as adult presentation. Dependent on fishing technique, leaders may vary from 3.0 to 8.0 meters in length and leader tippet as fine as 1.5 lb. (6X) may be required to successfully fish the smaller *Caenis* nymphs.

As mentioned earlier, *Callibaetis* nymph habitat includes submerged vegetation, large rock or woody debris areas generally to a depth of 7 meters. To effectively fish that depth, one must get the fly down and keep it within the zone of habitat. Depending on depth, this can be achieved either with a floating line, long leader and weighted nymph or with one of the sinking lines and an unweighted nymph. Again, the important point to remember is that the fly must be fished where the naturals are normally found. *Callibaetis* nymphs are active swimmers and their movement can be best represented by several short 3.0 to 8.0 cm. pulls of line followed by a brief pause.

The most intense feeding activity of the trout is triggered by the rise to the surface of emerging nymphs. This culminates in slashing rises as they feed on newly–emerged duns. The slow emergence–swim can be effectively imitated with either the intermediate or slow–sinking lines and unweighted nymphs. Depending on depth, both lines will allow the fly to be retrieved on an upward angle. The retrieve should consist of several medium fast hand twist movements followed by a pause of up to several seconds. Also effective is a floating line and sinking leader slightly longer than the depth of water being fished. This technique, used in conjunction with wind–drifting can also be extremely productive. Wind–drifting calls for casting at right angles or quartering to the wind and allowing the wave action to move the flyline and fly downwind. By varying the length of leader and using weighted or unweighted nymphs, this technique can cover virtually all emergence depths. When wind–drifting it is important to keep a tight line, as often a fish will hit and take out line immediately. Any loose coils of flyline in the boat may allow enough slack for the fish to shake the hook. At other times, the only detection of a strike is a slight movement or pull of the tip of the floating flyline. In this situation, the fish has just inhaled the fly and is swimming away not knowing he has taken an imitation. Once drag is felt, the trout will try to spit the fly out immediately. In both situations, the angler must be constantly watching the floating line and be quick to react.

Again, by watching the type of surface activity, the angler can determine whether the trout are taking nymphs subsurface or floating. Floating nymphs can be imitated by either treating nymph patterns with floatant or by tying patterns that incorporate bouyant material in the thorax or wingcase. A floating line is used in this situation and the fly is usually wind drifted or inched in very slowly. The natural at this point is just sitting in the surface film as the dun begins emerging from the dorsal part of the thorax.

Upon hatching, the dun will sit on the water for up to several minutes before flying off to shore. Often individual fish will move in a specific feeding pattern. The observant angler can anticipate this pattern and with an accurate cast present an artificial with success. Wind drifting dun imitations is also an excellent technique to use especially when surface activity is scattered. Patterns tied parachute style give good body silhouettes as well as having excellent floating qualities. Careful presentation and realistically-tied patterns are required to fool the often selective larger trout.

The spinner-fall also attracts feeding trout. Often the water will be covered with dead females with transparent wings lying flat on the surface. Spinner-falls usually occur under calm weather conditions thus necessitating long leaders and fine tippet sections. The most effective methods of spinner fishing include dead-drifting or watching for individual feeding fish and anticipating feeding locations. Imitations must have wings tied of translucent materials and also be tied flat so they ride flush on the water.

Special Conditions
With all types of lake flyfishing, the angler must be in control of the flyline and fly. When fishing mayflies it is very important to have a completely stationary boat. This means double-anchoring or having anchors down from both bow and stern of the boat. A sudden gust of wind will not cause unwanted movement of your boat and therefore your nymph or adult imitations.

The term "matching the hatch" was in fact developed from fishing mayfly imitations as trout can be extremely selective in terms of size, colouration and presentation.

Therefore, it's a good idea to carry an aquarium net and some small glass vials with you so that all phases of mayfly development can be collected and observed carefully for colour and size.

Perhaps the most difficult mayfly fishing conditions are a combination of bright sunlight and dead calm water conditions. A hatch may be in progress but the trout are very apprehensive when approaching the surface zone. Undoubtedly, the majority of fish will still be feeding on the emerging nymphs but in the deeper parts of the shoal. One should try the sinking line techniques rather than the surface or subsurface methods.

Under bright sunlight and clear water conditions, trout will often strike short at subsurface nymphs, floating emergers and duns. An angler's first reaction to a boil or slashing rise is to strike but in these instances, no contact is made. That is because these fish are drowning the fly first and then returning to pick it up. One should try, although it is very difficult, to let the fly sit through the first rise and then be prepared for a strike almost immediately after.

The information contained in this chapter will hopefully give you the basic knowledge of how to fish mayflies in lakes. The accompanying entomology profile will add additional life–cycle and identification information. With these, it is hoped that encountering future hatches will be enjoyable experiences.

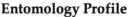

Entomology Profile

Common Name: Mayfly nymph, dun and spinner
Taxonomic Classification: Order Ephemeroptera,
   Family Baetidae (*Callibaetis* sp.)
   Family Caenidae (*Caenis* sp.)
   This profile discusses two specific mayfly families which are known to inhabit most Interior lakes of British Columbia.

Size Range: *Callibaetis* — 3–12 mm. nymph and adult excluding tails.

Caenis — 2–8 mm. nymph and adult excluding tails

Colouration: *Callibaetis* nymph — mottled olive tan dun and spinner — mottled grey to almost black body
Caenis nymph — light tan to medium brown dun and spinner — often a creamy white body

Preferred Habitat: *Callibaetis* nymphs are capable of living in very diverse habitats. They have been found in alpine lakes as high in elevation as 4000 metres and in sewage treatment ponds. Generally, their preferred habitat is among dense aquatic vegetation within relatively clear waters. They feed on detritus and vegetation and are most commonly found in depths of less than 7 metres. The nymphs are very active swimmers and can often be seen darting among the vegetation.

Callibaetis.

Caenis nymphs also inhabit the dense submerged vegetative growths in lakes but are not active swimmers. Often the nymphs will bury themselves in the bottom silt for additional protection. They feed as well on detritus and vegetation. Their small size makes them difficult to find even in lakes that are known to have good populations. Both *Callibaetis* and *Caenis* nymphs undergo numerous molts before "hatching" into the dun phase of the adult.

Caenis.

Availability to Trout: Nymphs are available year round but are most available to trout during their emergence–swim to the surface. Adults are available in both dun and spinner stages. Mayfly hatches do occur throughout the open water period but are most prolific during late May, June, and July.

Life Cycle: Contrary to common belief, the life cycle of mayflies is not complicated. It is basically a two part development from nymph to dun (the adult stage), and from dun to spinner (the reproductive stage).

Nymphs show signs of impending emergence when their fully developed wing pads darken in appearance. When ready to "hatch", the nymph takes air in through it's skin to help start the transformation and also aid in the swim to the surface. At the surface, the dun almost immediately crawls out of the nymphal skin, dries it's upright held wings and flies off. The hatching or emerging process usually occurs so quickly that the duns give the appearance of almost popping out of the water. It is only in conditions of very cool or humid weather that the emergence time is increased. The newly hatched duns or subimagoes are dull in appearance and have characteristically opague coloured wings. This stage can last up to 48 hours before the dun will shed it's outer skin and fly away as a spinner.

The spinner or imago form differs in appearance from the dun by having a glossy shine to the body and translucent colouration of the wings. The mayfly is now ready to mate. Females mate by flying into swarms of males who are hovering over water or land. A short time later the mated females return to the water to deposit their eggs. By flying low over the water she can dip her abdomen through the surface film and release the eggs. The eggs sink to the bottom to start a new generation. The female spinner having completed her role, falls onto the water's surface and dies. The male spinners suffer the same fate 1 to 2 days later.

Distinguishing Features: In general, Mayfly nymphs are easily distinguished from other invertebrate larvae by the presence of 2 or 3 slender elongated tails and the location of breathing gills along both sides of the abdomen.

Callibaetis duns are recognized by their *darkly speckled* opaque wings held upright over the body. Two or three long slender tails and prominent eyes are also features of the dun form. The final molt to the reproductive spinner stage is identified by translucent wings and a slender abdominal form.

Caenis duns, although almost minute in size are distinquished by their almost *solid white wings* and creamy brown body. The spinner form again has translucent wings and a much more slender body.

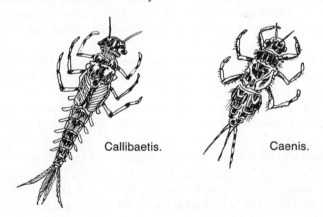

Callibaetis.   Caenis.

VIII
Damselfly . . . the Stillwater Darling

by Jim Crawford

Few insects are as pretty, or fly with the grace and beauty of the adult damselfly, and perhaps no insect has been written about as much over the centuries by poets and naturalists . . . But I must be honest . . . this is not one of my favorite bugs!

Damselflies are of the order Odonata, sub-order Zygoptera. In North America there are four distinct families, twenty-one genera, and over one hundred known species. Historically the name "dragonfly" has been applied to both dragons *and* damsels even though in their aquatic larval ("nymph") phase of development and as adults they do not resemble each other at all. Only in the very early larval stages might they be confused.

Damselflies go through an "incomplete" metamorphic life cycle of egg, larvae and adult. There is no pupal stage as with chironomids and sedges.

At all times during their normal two to three year aquatic nymphal life, damsels provide a good source of food for fish, and for larger predacious aquatic insects such as dragonflies and various water beetles. Generally shy, damsel nymphs tend to "hide in the weeds", venturing out only to attack smaller invertebrates on which they feed or to migrate. By their third year they may have gone through ten or twelve molts (called instars) gaining slightly in size with each. At maturity the nymph will measure only about 20 mm. in length.

In this discussion, we will concentrate on damsels around the Kamloops region. The most common *adult* in this region is the beautiful bright blue and black insect which identifies as Enallagma of the narrow–winged damselfly family. I have also seen, on occasion, violet coloured and tan ones which would be the male and female respectively of a close cousin, The Argia damsels.

Colours of the *nymphs* are normally shades of olive and this may vary with age and the effect of aquatic vegetation in which they live. For instance, as the nymphs grow with each moult, they usually become darker. Nymphs living in clear water with bright green weed indicative of that environment will take on brighter green bodies, whereas off–colored water such as caused by tannin will give them a more brown color. So take a look at the water and vegetation before you cast your damsel nymph and have a variety which run from dusty–mustard yellow to olive and brown.

Damsel Fly
Nymph.

When . . .? In the Northwest, damsels will start to move in May on the low warm lakes, and may not hatch off until September on some high lakes. And unlike dragons which must crawl along the bottom to their place of exit to hatch, damsels are fairly good (though slow) swimmers and will use anything handy to climb up when their time comes to emerge. Certainly all of us have experienced them clambering up anchor ropes and along boat gunwhales in search of a quiet place to attach themselves and begin final metamorphosis into the winged adult. A quick movement by the angler will send them scampering (literally!) over the edge and back into the water. But quiet repose may allow you to witness one of Nature's most wonderous transformations . . . the change from an insignificant little crawling, swimming creature into a magnificent, slender and graceful flying thing of beauty . . . I never get tired of watching and realizing I am being entrusted with the safety and protection of a totally defenseless life form during that brief moment of time. My role as protector is always well repaid . . .

In our Interior lakes, fishing with damsel nymph patterns a week or so prior to the actual hatch is often excellent. Bottom activity attracts attention as nymphs begin swimming in and around the weeds. When the final migration begins the dam–. sels swim up towards the surface and then level off just under it, heading shoreward. With legs straight out from each side they gyrate their segmented abdomens side to side in an effort

70

to swim. Progress is slow but effective, and frequent rest stops are necessary due to the vigorous labour. Any object encountered which allows them to climb up out of the water, such as a reed stalk, limb, anchor rope, etc., will do just fine.

June is the best month around Kamloops, but I don't pay much attention to damsels even though they are an important food source for fish in many lakes. Why don't I like them . . .? Well, many have heard my Stump Lake story, but for the record: I was driving from Peterhope Lake to Roche Lake in mid–June some years ago. It was one of those *very* rare days when the entire Merritt Plateau was absolutely calm, and as I drove along the south end of Stump Lake I could see fish moving everywhere among the reeds. I wasn't due at Roche until evening so the decision to stop was easy. In retrospect, I didn't realize just how big some of the fish I saw really were!

I had never fished Stump, even though I'd heard great stories about big fish, so the first little while was spent trying to figure out what they could be feeding on so near shore in the middle of the day. I was familiar with surface action on chironomids, mayflies, sedges, etc., and thought perhaps it might be sedges . . . but there were none. My only alternative was to row in near the reeds and have a look. The answer came quickly . . . *damsels* as thick as pollywogs were swimming among the rushes and thousands of dried nymph cases clung to the stems.

In my fly box were six beautiful damsels given to me by Jack Shaw in about 1975. I always intended to keep them since flies tied by Jack are so special. But here I was surrounded by fish gorging on damsel nymphs, and they were the only damsel patterns I had . . .

The result of my first cast was the sin of a pure rookie! I was using a floating line, twelve foot leader, and 3 lb. tippet. I picked a big sloshing boil and put the little damsel right in it. The line tightened instantly and I set up . . . With 10 lb. tippet I'd have broken the fish's neck . . . with the tippet I had on, it never even felt the slight ping.

My second cast was about the same. I could see a fish moving towards me along the edge of the reeds about thirty feet away. I cast in front of it and started a slow retrieve. Its mouth opened, and again I broke on the set up. But this time I could see the fish shaking its head. As it got closer I became aware it was a *very* large fish, and at last realized what I had just been into.

Fish continued to boil all along the edge of the reeds as I changed to heavier tippet and tied on a third damsel. With much apprehension I laid out a good cast and promised myself I wouldn't set up the next time . . . I didn't have to. This fish sucked in the fly, realized a mistake had been made and immediately headed for deep water. Line jerked from the floor of my boat and as the last coil came up it folded neatly over the handle of my reel and the run was over in a split second! Disgusted with myself, I tied on the fourth damsel. It was several casts before another big fish blasted out across the shallows with my fly. He just "went" in a wide sweep around the front of my boat, and never stopped! I had over fifty yards of backing, and a thirty-five yard fly line. It is really heart-stopping to watch backing strip off your reel, especially right near the end, and wonder if the line is tied to the reel or will the fish take everything? That day I didn't take a chance . . . I broke him off with about twenty feet to spare.

My fifth damsel met an unlikely end; I hit the boat with it while casting and broke the hook point, and the sixth went the way of number four in a scorching run and jump that left me shaking.

It had taken thirty minutes and I was finished for the day! I tried several other patterns, but the fish knew better. In an hour they moved out, it quieted down, and I headed on up to Roche.

That evening in the lodge I told my sad story to Hal Janssen. At that point in life I had been fly fishing for twenty years: I *knew* better! My friend just laughed and we made plans to go back down there together the next day. But a storm blew in overnight and Hal had to leave for home in California the following day, so we never did fish Stump. I went on to Hatheume Lake for a week of the great chironomid fishing of those years and two weeks later I received a letter from Hal telling me about the 10 lb. Kamloops he released at Stump on the way home . . . on a damsel! I'm sure I cried. Anyway, maybe now it's clear why damselflies are *not* one of my favorite bugs . . .?

In any event, they certainly should be used. Pick a pattern which sinks a bit and fish it with a dry line. Neutral density sinking lines or a #1 slow sink-tip work all right also . . . Move the fly with fairly long, *slow* pulls just under the surface, stopping once in awhile for a few seconds to simulate the "resting" period. The hit, as described by Jack Shaw, can be "as soft as a puff of wind, or as vicious as a snapping dog!" I know all about that, and "just in case", I now carry about two dozen damsels in a private section of my fly box.

The *adult* stage of the damsel is not really worth considering as an important pattern. As mentioned earlier, it is such a beautiful and graceful flying creature perhaps fish would rather watch it than eat it . . . There are times though, and I have witnessed them on rare occasion, when fish do actively feed on the adult. In fact, at certain lakes in the Monte Hills area, fish feed on them every summer. Two fishing partners, Bill Turanski and Barry Blois from Vernon, have created an adult pattern which is very effective at times like that. It's tied entirely with polypro yarn, is extremely light weight, and with a bit of floatant, rides like a cork! Fish take it with the same splashy attack as on travelling sedges. But even so, I don't have an adult pattern and feel I wouldn't use it if I did . . .

As obvious as it sounds the real key to success with damsels is recognizing when fish are feeding on nymphs. Usually it will be late morning or early afternoon on a warm day and you suddenly become aware of damsels flying all around you. Head for the nearest shoal and watch along the edges of reeds for fish moving just under the surface. Then, as you cast, remember my day on Stump Lake . . . and be gentle.

Entomology Profile
Common Name: Damselfly Nymph
Taxonomic Classification: Order Odonata, Suborder Zygo-
    ptera
Size Range: Up to 30 mm. in length.
Colouration: Various shades of yellow, green and brown dependent on habitat they are living in.

Preferred Habitat: Good damselfly populations are almost always associated with lakes having abundant aquatic vegetation such as Chara, potamogeton and milfoil.
    Emergent vegetation including sedge grasses and rushes along the lake shore are also important. Nymphs inhabit the dense mats of vegetation for both protection and sources of food. Their diet includes insect larvae, shrimp and zooplankton. They are capable swimmers using their three fanlike tails (actually gills) to propel them through the water.

Availability to Trout: As nymphs year round but most sought after during their emergence swim to shore. Adults that unintentionally land on the water and egg laying females are sometimes actively sought after by trout.

Life Cycle: The nymphal stage of damselflies can be as short as six months or as long as one year. During development they will go through several instars or molts before being ready to emerge as an adult. At the appropriate time the nymph will begin swimming to the surface in search of some vegetation protruding above the water. After crawling out of the water the nymphal skin dries and splits along the back allowing the adult to crawl out.

After mating, females return to the lake to deposit eggs either on the surface of the water which then sink to the bottom or at the base of emergent vegetation.

Damselflies emerge throughout the open water period but are most prolific during June and July.

Distinguishing Features: Damselfly nymphs are easily recognized by their slender elongated body ending with three distinct tails which are actually their respiratory organs.

These nymphs also have a distinct swimming motion of undulating in a sideways (sinosoidal) fashion. Adult damselflies can be distinguished from dragonflies by their much smaller slender bodies. Also when at rest the damselfly folds its wings parallel over the top of the abdomen while dragonflies maintain their wings extended out away from the body.

IX
Dragons: The Bottom Predator

by *Alf Davy*

When I first started to fish fly patterns which I thought imitated dragonfly nymphs, I really had no idea what a live dragonfly nymph looked like. For a couple of years I tied up flies that I thought must be accurate replicas. I was fairly successful trolling these patterns, but casting with them did not produce any fish.

I began to read books and articles on fly fishing and entomology and a whole new experience opened up for me. I now had a better idea about the insect I should be trying to imitate. The next few winters at my fly tying table proved to be a rewarding experience in creating a whole variety of dragonfly patterns.

After many patterns I was ready to attack any lake with my new–found knowledge. My dragonfly pattern had the essential features of a dragon nymph. It was two to five centimeters in length, it was the right bulbous shape, it displayed various shades of green and it was weighted to get it down on the bottom where the fish were. I was successful, right? Wrong! I caught the odd fish but there were more problems than fish. The weighted fly proved dangerous to cast and whenever it hit the boat the noise would scare away the fish. If it hit the caster or a fellow flyfisher, it would almost knock him out of the boat. You could hear the fly hit a jacket from one hundred meters away. As if that were not bad enough, the fly was like a dredge on the bottom with all the weeds it brought up. As long as I did not let the fly sink too deep, I might catch a fish or two by the count-down method of casting and counting and then retrieving, each time counting longer until I started to catch bottom.

That winter it was back to the books. I again went over what I was trying to imitate in the natural nymph. I had learned that dragon nymphs are divided into two groups; those that hide and climb in the weeds and those that are mud and bottom dwellers. I would need to have two patterns then, because the shape, size and colour of these two groups of dragons are very different.

Colour, Shape and Movement

The weed dwellers or Darners are darker in colour than the mud dragons and can be black, dark brown and dark olive to light green in colour. The mud nymphs or Red Shoulder dragons are more tan coloured. The lake bottom colour and vegetation must be taken into account when matching either species as they will try and blend with their natural surroundings to escape the eyes of their natural enemies, diving birds and trout. As a rule, I tie light coloured patterns for light bottom lakes and darker patterns for dark bottom lakes.

Carey.

However, surrounding colour is not the only factor as illustrated by the following story about a day's fishing at Salmon Lake in the Douglas Lake region of B.C. I was using a darker olive Carey pattern one day without very much success, even though the fly in the past had been very good for me. There was one fisherman that was having very good success and when I asked him what colour his fly was he replied that it was light green. I happened to have a nymph pattern in light green and tied it on, and after only a couple of casts, I landed a nice fish. I spooned it to see what it was feeding on and it was just full of dragon nymphs that were a light watery-green in colour. This perplexed me because I thought dragon nymphs were dark in colour. It was not until sometime later that I came to understand that dragons molt and change skins as they grow larger. Each time they molt, they are a very light colour for a few days until the new skin hardens and darkens. That day fish were selectively feeding on the molting nymphs.

The weed dragon nymphs (Darner) are longer in length than mud dwellers. I have seen some up to nine centimeters

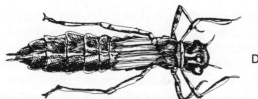

Darner.

but five centimeters is more normal. The insect has a large head and eyes and its abdomen is narrow to start with and gets wider until just after three quarters of its length where it quickly narrows. The mud dwellers are much shorter and more stubby. Both have six legs but the weed crawler has long thin ones for crawling on the weeds, while the mud nymph (Red Shoulder) has short, thick legs for digging.

Red Shoulder.

Dragon nymphs can move rapidly for short periods of time by ejecting water from their posterior orifice. They spurt quickly in five to eight centimeter bursts, but usually only when frightened. Most of the time they move very little and tend to let their food come to where they are hiding, or they will move very slowly while searching for food.

Fly Design

The need to be on the bottom with a slow retrieve was what had caused my problems the previous year. I was now determined to create a nymph pattern that I could retrieve slowly along the bottom without hanging up on weeds and sticks. I kept asking myself the question, "What fly tying material will give me bouyancy?" Tying on closely packed deer hair like that found on certain dry flies gave me my answer. Using deer hair solved two problems: It gave me the floatation I needed to keep the fly off the bottom and it was easy to shape the dragon nymphs's body by clipping the deer hair. I could then dub on seal fur in any colour I wanted. (A point here is to make sure you clip the deer hair close between hook and point so that the hook gap is as wide as possible for better hooking.

77

I tied my first flies and looked at the result. I could still visualize the point of the hook catching weeds, so I tied stiff moose mane along the bottom of the fly as a beard, extending it just past the point of the hook. I tried moving the fly slowly over a pencil and the moose hackle bumped the fly up and over the object without the point of the hook catching. Now I was ready for those dragon nymph–eating trout.

The fly did exactly as I envisioned. I could move it as slowly along the bottom as I wanted and it would not hang up on the weeds. I gave the fly the name, "Bottom Walker" and it proved to be an exceptional pattern. It will not be a viable commercial pattern because of the time required to tie it, but for those who can tie or have friends that do, it is a worthwhile pattern. I used the fly for a year in New Zealand and it was just as effective there. I also use this idea on my All–Black leech pattern and my shrimp, or any pattern I want to slowly retrieve on the bottom.

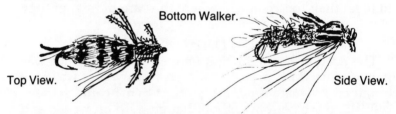

Bottom Walker.

Top View.

Side View.

My fishing friend and companion, Jim Crawford, took this weed–crawling pattern, shaped it to look like Jack Shaw's seal fur Gomphus mud-dwelling nymph pattern, added some pheasant tail legs on either side, eliminated the moose mane, and it became the "Gomphus", our best pattern for imitating mud nymphs. The beauty of the Gomphus pattern is that the deer hair is the same colour as the natural.

'Gomphus'.

Top View.

Method of Fishing

There are two ways to fish dragonfly patterns. Anchor near a shoal or drop-off and cast a sinking line into the deep water. By the counting method, wait until you think your fly is on the bottom, then slowly retrieve it. Move the fly inch by inch with frequent pauses in the retrieve. Avoid long quick pulls as that will drive the fly down into the weeds. Just slowly walk the fly in. When a fish takes this nymph, they usually just suck it in as they pick it off the bottom. You may only feel a slight tightening of the line. Softly raise your rod from a position of pointing at the fly to a position about waist high. If the contact continues or if you feel movement, 'strike'! Often it is only weed but just as often it's a fish.

I came upon the second method of retrieving the Bottom Walker by chance. I was fishing Jocko Lake outside of Kamloops on the long May weekend a few years ago, with about ninety other boats. In three hours of fishing in the morning, I had seen only one fish caught by a troller. I was fishing along the shore with two rods hooked up, a dry line for chironomids and a "Hi D" for my dragon nymph. I had spent the morning either dry line chironomid fishing towards shore in one to three meters of water or casting into the deep part of the lake with the "Hi D", but all to no avail. I had just retrieved a cast from deep water with the dragon nymph when I noticed some fish moving along the shore. I cast inwards towards the shallows with my wet line and since the water was only one meter deep and weedy, I had to retrieve very fast to keep from hanging up. For the next two hours, I had a bite on almost every cast and even though some boats moved in on me and started to cast, it was only the fast retrieve on the dark olive green dragon that took fish.

I now had a second method of retrieving my pattern: cast towards the shallows from deep water, let the fly sink by the count-down method, and bring it in quickly along the bottom. To achieve the movement I wanted of a dragon nymph expelling water and spurting along, I used hand strips of twenty to twenty-five centimeters or quick figure eight weaves with my hand. The fish will usually hit the fly very hard as they are able to get a run at it and will usually hook themselves on the take.

For me, these fly patterns and methods work. But to give you some idea of how complex or simple it all can be, I will point out that in my fly fishing club, there are a couple of excellent fly fishermen who have very good results with two entirely different patterns! One uses a Felt Hat Dragon and the other uses a good attractor of seal or chenille. The Felt Hat Dragon is a fly that has its basic shape cut from a piece of felt hat and then is doubled over with seal of various colours and fished on the bottom. The attractor (Hatheume Nymph) is simply dubbed seal fur, or chenille, in light or dark olive body, wide tinsel ribbing and short sparse blue-green pheasant hackle. I used this pattern very successfully this last spring and fall with a floating line in shallow water with a slow retrieve. Then there is Jack Shaw's pattern tied of seal and clipped to the right shape, which really works for him.

Hatheume Nymph

Shaw's Nymph

Clearly, then, there is no one pattern that will do all things. When you think you have solved all the problems, the next season can humble you. There are a lot of variables, like the correct retrieve, the correct size and colour and the right knowledge, such as knowing that nymphs are smaller in the fall than in the spring when they hatch into adults. Fish feed more selectively at times and then the fly fishermen must come up with more exact representations of the natural. The challenge is always with us.

Gomphus.

Darner.

Entomology Profile

Common Name: Dragonfly Nymph

Taxonomic Classification: Order Odonata, Suborder Anisoptera

Family Aeschnidae (*Anax*, Darners)

Family Gomphidae (*Gomphus*, Red Shouldered)

This profile discusses the two most common families of dragonflies found in Interior lakes.

Size Range: Darners — up to 60 mm. in length

Red Shouldered — up to 35 mm. in length

Colouration: The larger Darner nymph is found in a wide variety of aquatic habitat and thus has a wide range of colouration. Most common colours include shades of green, brown, black and even red. The Red Shouldered nymph tends to be lighter in colouration including shades of yellow, olive green and light brown.

Preferred Habitat: Dragonfly nymphs are basically bottom dwellers where they find both food and shelter from predators. The Darners are found in a wider range of lake types from the darker water lily pad lakes to the clear white marl shoal lakes. They actively seek out food such as shrimp, insect larvae and small fish. Darners are excellent swimmers using a water jet propulsion system through the tip of the abdomen. Red Shouldered nymphs have more specific habitat requirements and are generally found in clear water lakes of higher pH, shallow depths and good growths of chara vegetation. These nymphs obtain food by laying in wait and ambushing their prey. Although they have a similar propulsion system to the Darners, the red shouldered nymph is much more sedentary in nature. They are often found covered in algae growth and half buried in the bottom sediments or well hidden in a mass of *chara* vegetation.

Availability to Trout: Year round but most actively sought as nymphs migrate to shoreline vegetation in the spring to emerge as adults. Adult dragonflies that have fallen onto the water and become trapped in the surface film are occasionally fed on by trout.

Life Cycle: Dragonflies have an extended nymphal development involving up to 12 instars or molts and requiring up to 4 years to complete. The wing pads of nymphs characteristically darken in colouration just prior to their emergence as an adult. The "developed" nymphs migrate to shore seeking out emergent vegetation to crawl up on and complete the change to adult. As the nymphal skin dries off a split develops running from the head along it's back. The adult crawls out of the nymphal skin and immediately begins pumping blood through it's crumpled wings and abdomen. It may take several hours before the adult is fully formed and able to fly away. After mating the female returns to the lake and while flying low over the water releases eggs which sink to the lake bottom. Dragonflies emerge throughout the open water period but are probably more abundant during May through August.

Distinguishing Features: The Darner nymph is long and slender in shape and usually found hiding under logs, rocks or attached to submerged vegetation. It is an active swimmer and found in a wide range of lake types.

Darner.

The *Gomphus* or Red shouldered nymph is short and stubby

81

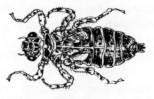

Gomphus.

in shape with long spider-like legs. Their entire body is often covered in hairlike projections which acts as a base for algae to grow from. These nymphs are more sedentary in nature and are usually found well hidden in submerged vegetation. Adults of this family have a distinct red shoulder patch on their wings.

X

Caddis —
Pre-Emergence
Techniques

by Doug Porter

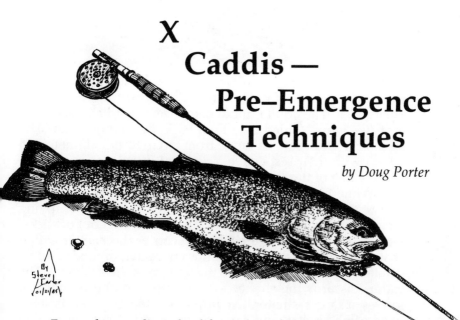

By understanding the life cycles of the Caddisfly, the knowledgeable flyfisher can greatly increase the chance of success by fishing larval or pupal imitations prior to or immediately after major sedge hatches. Waiting for a sedge hatch can be exasperating. It's like waiting for grunion or salmon runs; you know that someday they'll appear, and it's this anticipation that keeps you coming back year after year. Some years it's very frustrating to watch the first sedges of the season being ignored, either because there are too few of them, or the fish haven't found them yet or the weather is lousy.

But if you hit it right, you'll find that nothing triggers the feeding response of rainbow trout in lakes more than a Caddisfly (sedge) hatch. On the surface, sedges prompt explosive rises from larger fish which, at most other times, seem to reject all attempts to prove their existence in a given body of water. But while dry fly fishing is an imitation of adult sedges and may provide the most exciting action, it is not necessarily the most productive method for catching and releasing a lot of fish.

Caddisflies belong to the insect order Trichoptera which contains over twenty families. They have a complete metamorphosis, going from egg to larva to pupa and finally adult stages. The larval and pupal stages of the sedge are aquatic and are readily available to the subsurface foraging trout with the larvae providing food for the fish for up to two years and

Adult sedge.

Larvae case.

Larvae.

the pupae being a prime source of food during periods of emergence. The adults, moth-like insects with characteristic tent-like wings folded over their back, live out of water. The size of the adult sedges range from ten to forty millimeters in length with their respective larval and pupal stages approximately that of the adult.

While two families of Caddisflies have free-swimming larvae, the rest are case builders with each family occupying old snailcases or building its own unique shelter out of sticks, weeds, grains of sand or pebbles. It carries this shelter with it as it forages across the lake bottom in search of food. Caddis "trails" are often seen across the bottom in the shallows. The caddis discards the shelter as it outgrows it and rebuilds or locates a larger shelter. At pupation, the larva seals itself inside this shelter and later emerges as a free-swimming pupa.

Caddis larvae are segmented and worm-like in appearance, having dark heads and long legs which are used in crawling over the bottom. Only the head and legs protrude from the cases and are quickly withdrawn if they are alarmed. They range from white or cream-coloured to pale or bright green for the free swimming species. They are particularly vulnerable to predators like trout as they leave one shelter in search of another.

Generally Caddis larvae occupy the littoral (shallow, weedy) zone of any lake and can be found from the shallow waters right down to the maximum depth that light can penetrate. Rocky shoals and outcrops provide cover for some species and casting over these areas can often produce some exciting fishing when trout forage there. Usually early morning and evening will provide the most action in the shallows (up to three meters in depth) while deeper water is where the fish will most likely be found through the strong, light hours.

Because each casemaker uses materials found along the bottom area it inhabits, an effective imitation would consist of colours compatible with the types of bottom over which it is fished. The Half Back or Full Back flies can produce good results when fished along marl bottoms where larvae use small, dark pieces of hollow reeds for their shelters. The Werner Shrimp or any other deer hair back shrimp in shades

Half-back.

Shrimp.

84

of green can be productive when fished slowly over various weedbeds. A dark green Carey heavily dubbed with seal's fur forming a tubular shaped, clipped body is also effective when fished deep over weedbeds that are along drop-offs.

Carey.

Success with these patterns usually depends on the fly being fished slowly right on the bottom. When fished on the bottom with a sinking line, flies constructed of hollow deer hair, such as a Tom Thumb, allow the fly to be fished just above the weeds. An added advantage of this fly is that, with wear, it becomes ragged and more attractive to the fish. When the deer hair splits, it leaves broken ends which more typically represents the cases built by the larvae.

Tom Thumb.

The Caddis pupa is a relatively short-lived stage in the sedge's life cycle. After the pupa matures, it chews its way out of the case and swims to the surface. The sedge is most vulnerable during this stage, since it is highly visible to the fish as it rises from the bottom to the surface and remains suspended there for a short period struggling to break the surface tension. Quite often the trout will key (select) to just the pupa, and not go after the adults on the surface, especially during periods of intense sunlight, high surface water temperatures or a rough surface caused by winds.

Pupa.

Different species of sedges hatch from mid-June through September in the Interior lakes. The size of the Caddisfly generally determines the trout's response to them. The smaller sedges are quite often ignored by the larger fish. However, the larger sedges (over twenty-five millimeters) generally draw the interest of bigger fish if there are many emerging. It is the hatch of big sedges that attracts the flyfisher as well as the trout. The chance of hooking larger fish when the big bugs are out is really good. Many keep diaries of these emergences and plan their fishing trips to coincide with the sedge hatches.

Adult Caddis Fly.

Depending on the lake's elevation, the hatches which elicit the best response from the fish occur from mid-June in lower elevation lakes to mid-July in higher elevation lakes. The timing of these hatches can vary slightly from year to year depending on water temperature and weather patterns. The first sedges of the year emerge from the shallow water; then progress to the deeper water over the season.

Most of the major hatches of the larger sedges occur in the early afternoon with the pupae rising from as shallow as half a meter of water to as deep as ten meters. Large trout can be found during peak emergence periods right up in the shallows even during the intense light hours.

Being where the insects are emerging greatly increases the chance of catching a trout. Watch for splashy rises, swooping birds and sedges fluttering on the water. Since emergences may occur sporadically over a number of days, keep the spot in mind and make note of the time of day the adult insects were seen emerging. Look for their discarded pupal cases floating on the surface. Their absence may indicate that the adults observed were returning to deposit eggs. They are mainly nocturnal, generally spending the daylight hours concealed in the cover along the shore and laying their eggs in the evening.

Patterns.   Pupae.

Once you have located the area where a particular species of sedge is emerging, choose the appropriate line for presenting the pupal imitation. A floating, slow sink or sink tip is best for water up to five meters in depth and a sink tip or medium sink line for water over five meters. Using a Knouff Lake Special or a green Carey in sizes approximating that of the pupa, let the fly sink to the bottom and retrieve it in short jerks followed by a long pull of about half a meter. Pause for about five seconds, then repeat the process. Retrieves can be varied but this one works fairly well. A dry line can be dead-drifted (cast out at an angle to the wind and drifted until it is straight downwind). When using this technique, occasionally give the line a few short jerks during the drift stage to impart life-like movement to the fly. Longer leaders of up to six meters in length should be used.

The pupal imitation can be fished before and after the insects actually hatch, or at times when the fish are not taking the adults off the surface. You can greatly increase the fishing time and the chance of success by having two rods in the boat;

one with a sinking line for fishing the pupa and the other with a Tom Thumb on a dry line to imitate the adult when the fish start rising.

Dry flies for sedges will provide short periods of excitement but pupal imitations will provide for longer periods of fishing and a greater chance of success. The well-rounded sedge fisher will always be equipped to fish both pupae and adult sedge imitations.

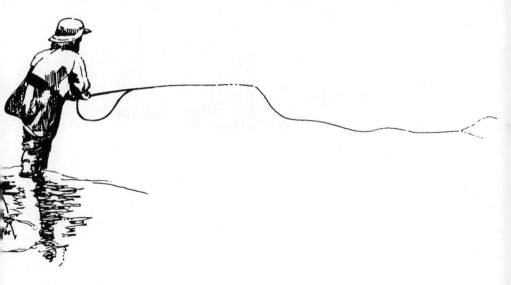

XI
Tom Thumb: The Dry For All Seasons

by Ralph Shaw

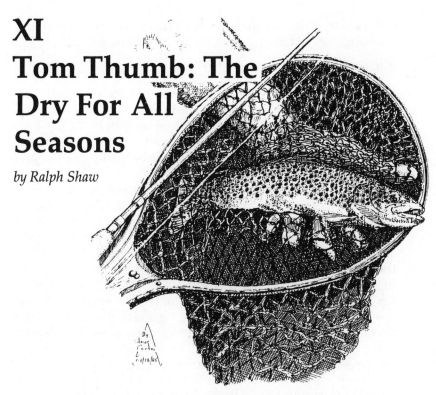

As I sit at my desk writing this it is easy to slip into memories of fantastic fish and fishing connected with the Tom Thumb . . .

I remember superb evenings on Jocko Lake where I regularly hooked and landed trout to four and five pounds on tiny #16 Tom Thumbs.

And I remember fishing Ernest Lake with my good friend Wilf Pelly when we hit fish after fish with #14 Tom Thumbs in a ripple along the edge of the marl beds.

History

I do not know just when the first Tom Thumb was tied; history isn't very clear on that. But I do know it had to be prior to the early forties. I have in my collection of flies an unopened package of Tom Thumbs that were tied under the Hardy Brothers label in England about 1940. They are essentially the same fly we tie today, except the hair is probably European Red Deer.

Also, Andy Anderson, who lived in Kamloops for many years, fished the Thompson River between Savona and Ashcroft from the early fifties to the mid–seventies. The *only* fly Andy ever used was the Tom Thumb! He tied it in three different styles to match the various hatches during the year. I have samples of his original flies and they are unique!

Tying

If I were limited to just one material from which to tie flies, I would have to choose deer hair. There are many flies that can be tied out of deer hair, but to me the Tom Thumb is the most important. The only material used in tying the Tom Thumb, besides hook, thread, and head cement, is deer hair! It is easy to tie and therefore ideal for the beginning fly tier and flyfisher.

Deer hair is very easy to come by for most people in B.C. But a word of caution; not all deer hair is the same. An early season deer has the best hair for Tom Thumbs. It will be of more even lengths which is essential for tying neat, well-balanced flies. If you are going to tie very large deer hair flies, then late October or November hair is best. It is long and ideally suited for big muddler minnows, etc. but not too good for Tom Thumbs because it is very uneven. If you have to use uneven hair for your Tom Thumbs, a good trick is to pinch the tip ends together and pull out the longer pieces. This leaves you with fairly even hair that will be adequate. Even hair tips can be achieved with a tying device called a ''stacker''.

Preparing your own deer hide is a simple process: flesh the hide carefully, salt well with picking salt, stretch it out and nail it to a wall or frame. In a couple of months you will have a lifetime supply of hair with plenty to trade with fellow fly tiers.

Hook selection is a key ingredient to consistently hooking fish with a Tom Thumb. Most commercially tied Tom Thumbs are tied on ''standard'' length hooks. I rarely tie on hooks less than 1x long, and frequently I use 2x long. The following illustrations show why I prefer the longer hooks.

Standard Pattern.

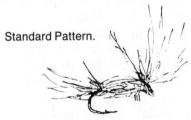

Note how the *hair* at the back of the fly extends well back of the hook point. This is a well balanced fly and will generate just as many strikes as the fly in our next illustration . . . but will result in far fewer hookups.

90

Longer shanked hook.

Here we have tied the same neatly balanced fly but have used a longer shanked hook. Now the point and barb of the hook extend beyond the end hair resulting in a great many more hookups. Very simple, but most effective.

When tying the fly use strong black or grey monocord (fine and very strong) thread. In order to tie a good Tom Thumb the body must be tied down tightly so it won't twist or come apart easily. With a properly tied Tom Thumb you should be able to catch and play at least a dozen fish.

Techniques

Methods of fishing the Tom Thumb vary with the type of insect you are trying to imitate. Essentially the Tom Thumb is a dry fly and is fished as such. Having said that, however, I must admit there are times when a beatup or trimmed down Tom Thumb will get spectacular results when fished on a sinking line to represent a shrimp, a dragonfly nymph or sedge larvae. But normally it is used to match a hatch on the surface.

Sedges: One of the most exciting ways to fish this fly is to imitate traveller sedges just after they emerge as adults and are moving rapidly across the surface of the water. You must move the fly fast with good bursts of speed and actually create a wake. It is essential the fly be kept dry. The real excitement comes when a big trout rolls and slashes at your sedge, ''confusing'' it, then returns to take it in a second round. It is a test of nerves and timing not to strike on that first roll. Leave the Tom Thumb sitting quietly until the lunker comes back and gulps it down.

There is no greater thrill than when you hold onto that moment of high excitement between the explosive first roll and the sound take. That is Tom Thumb fishing at a real high!

Most of the time I use a #10 or #12 Tom Thumb, tied on a #9671 Mustad for this type of fishing. And my flies are tied with the front hackles straight up or tilted slightly forward for better balance and good visible profile.

Mayflies: A "Slim" Tom Thumb can be tied to represent hatching mayflies. It is especially effective when there is a light ripple on the water. Use a #14–2x hook, long leader, and drop your fly gently on the surface. The trout will do the rest.

Frequently during the day or in the evening a good hatch will occur next to a reed bed in shallow water. Again with a slight ripple or even in a brisk breeze you can have amazing results. Cast your Tom Thumb right to the edge of the tullies and either leave it there or slowly bring it out into open water. Classic surface rises can be the expected result.

Chironomids: (Midges) Depending on the size of chironomidae which are hatching, I use #14, #16 or #18 Tom Thumbs, tied on #9672 Mustad Hooks. This type of fishing requires long leaders and long casts, usually out in open water where the insects are emerging. A slight ripple makes fishing easier and usually more productive. Simply cast to feeding fish and let your fly rest. The take is usually a quiet sip.

It is really difficult to estimate the size of feeding fish when they are on chironomids. Very large fish will take your fly the same way as small ones, so learn to set your hook *lightly* or be prepared to lose a lot of flies.

A second type of Tom Thumb chironomid fishing that presents a real challenge is the late evening rise. Midge hatches occur almost every evening on many of our lakes. The water is frequently dead calm and the fish are just dimpling. Food is very abundant and the fish are selective. I have had many thrilling evenings using a #16 and a long light leader.

Sometimes the fish move in small schools and are very shy. You must cast well ahead of moving fish and quietly wait for results. Often with this type of fishing you'll have the lake to yourself with only the loons, owls, coyotes and stars as company. It is a wonderful way to spend an evening just putting your soul in touch with the earth.

I should also mention for the benefit of those who are unable to cast a fly or who just wish to troll a fly, there is another very effective way to fish with a Tom Thumb: tie a large #8 on a floating line and troll it way back from the stern of your boat. Move slowly over weed beds and shoals and along drop-offs where large sedges may be travelling. Use a strong leader and make certain your rod is secure in the boat because some very large trout are taken in this manner, especially just as the sun is setting.

Try the Tom Thumb. It is my favorite dry fly and has the following endearing qualities:
1. It is easy to tie
2. The material is cheap and abundant
3. It catches fish under many conditions

Entomology Profile
Common Name: Caddisfly, sedge
Taxonomic Classification: Order Trichoptera

Size Range: 4–40 mm. in length for all life stages (larva, pupa, adult

Colouration: larva — shades of brown, green and yellow (almost all species construct cases in the larval stage for protection)
pupa — similar to larva but in some species brighter shades of green are observed
adult — green, yellow, browns for body colours while wings are tan to dark grey

Preferred Habitat: The aquatic environment is most import-ant to the caddisfly larva. Up to two years are spent in this stage as the larva is constantly growing and rebuilding its case. Larvae are commonly found crawling among dense growths of vegetation such as chara, potamageton and milfoil. Here they find shelter and sources of food which includes detritus, vegetation and other small invertebrates. Because of this preferred habitat, most Caddis larvae are found in depths of 7 metres or less.

Availability to Trout: Larvae are an available food source year round. However, Caddis are most sought after during pupal swim to surface, when adult is emerging from pupal skin, and as an adult when sitting or running across the surface of the lake. In the Interior of British Columbia most Caddis hatches occur during June and July, dependent on lake elevation. (The higher the elevation the later in the season is the hatch.)

Life Cycle: Caddis have a complete metamorphosis involving a larva, pupa and adult stage. This differs from dragon and damselflies as the adult emerges directly from the nymph or larva. The caddis larva may molt up to 5 times over a one or two year period dependent on species. After each molt the larva is required to build a new case. At some point in development the larva stops feeding, seals it's case and begins the transformation into the pupa. This is completed for most species in about 3 weeks. The pupa then cuts itself free of the case and swims to the surface. Reaching the surface, a fully formed adult crawls out of the pupal skin. The adult rests on the water for a few brief seconds in order to dry its wings which are held upright over its body. Once dried the wings are folded tent-like over the back and the adult almost immediately begins running across the surface film in an attempt to get airborne.

Mating occurs on land or water. Females release strands of eggs (often brightly coloured) by lowering her abdomen beneath the surface film as she either scurries or flies across the water. Egg laying often occurs in the evenings as females take advantage of the cover offered by poorer light conditions.

Distinguishing Features: Caddis larvae are easily recognized by the cases they build. Identification of some families can be accomplished by the type of construction and materials used. Several families do not build cases and larvae are ''free living'', however most of these are found in the river environment.

Caddis pupae are identified by a set of long antennae which extend to the tip of the abdomen. As well, the third pair of legs are elongated and oar-like in design to help propel the pupa through the water. Features that help distinguish adult caddis from terrestrial moths include the lack of suck-ing mouth parts and a prominent pair of antennae which are long and slender rather than short and feathery.

XII
Water Boatman (Corixa) — Stillwater Speeder

by Jim Crawford

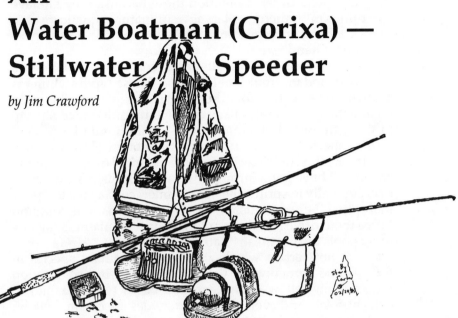

It's been over ten years since I first sat on Jocko Lake in my canoe and watched in wonder as fish moved all around the lake–edge in swift arching jumps. Out in deep water where I was fishing chironomids with friend and mentor, Jack Shaw, the fish would have nothing to do with us. Signaling my intentions to Jack, I paddled over to the big shoal on the south side of the lake.

It only took a moment to see what was happening: water boatmen, small air-breathing insects which live underwater, were bursting out of their chara weed cover, swimming to the surface to capture a bubble of air in the specialized pocket of tiny hairs on their abdomen, and heading swiftly back down, swimming in jerky, erratic spurts. Fish were picking them off just as they made the turn at the surface. What followed in the next hour was glorious . . . I took fish after fish, up to six pounds, and ended the day outfishing Jack Shaw! (To this day it remains the *only* time that has happened . . .!)

Corixa bug.

The family Corixidae, commonly called water boatmen, constitutes the largest single group of water bugs in North America with over one hundred species. They belong to the order Hemiptera which has other such notable members as Notonectidae or backswimmers, and Nepidae or water scor-

95

pions. Close cousins are the giant water beetles, Dytiscidae of the Coleoptera order. I mention these because they all have two things in common: as larvae or immature aquatic insects, fish love them; and these bugs bite! Don't pick up any of these with a bare hand . . .

During their one-year life cycle, corixa are available as a source of food for trout, but little else. These rapid swimmers are just a bit too quick for other predacious insects. They feed on aquatic invertebrates like scuds (commonly called shrimp in B.C., though they aren't, really), chironomid larvae and pupae, snails, leeches, and a variety of other minute animal life. By the time they reach their size potential of about 10mm., corixa will have gone through five molts or instars. At maturity, generally in spring or early summer, corixa take to the air in nuptual flight and disburse over wide areas. It is common to see them drive headlong onto wet pavement or into swimming pools during these ''hatches.''

I'm not certain which are the predominant species in B.C. — and certainly the fish don't care — but colouration ranges from yellow–brown mottled backs (wing casing) to rich chocolate and even black. Undersides are cream, yellow, and I have even seen soft blue–green. Undoubtedly water chemistry and vegetation play a part in colour, as it usually does with most aquatic species.

Patterns should have two distinct features: water boatmen have two long oar–like legs, which are highly functional as swimmers, protruding at right angles to their body (your fly should have these); also these insects carry their air supply with them in the form of a bubble tucked up under the abdomen. (This bubble is shiny, therefore your fly should have a short piece of silver mylar plastic or tinsel wrapped into the pattern that will give off a sparkle representing the bubble.) Tiny as corixa are, those two features are significant!

Corixa bug.

Here in the B.C. Interior, spring and early summer are usually the best times to use corixa, and in some years fall can be good also. Often it is the first insect of any significance to move right after ice–off. Fish moving in head–to–tail arches along the surface is a sure indicator they are feeding on boatmen . . .

One spring Alf Davy and I took our families on a weekend outing to Minnie Lake near the Douglas Lake cattle ranch. It was in the years when Minnie held monster Kamloops, before a summer drawdown of the water supply (for hayfields) caused a total fish kill and seriously damaged aquatic invertebrate populations. Today the lake is virtually barren and the grounds closed as the entire area has been set aside as a migratory bird sanctuary . . .

The weekend began well enough. Our four kids pitched-in and did a general clean-up of the camp area while Alf and I arranged campers and unloaded boats. By evening we were rowing to the far end of the lake into a steady breeze.

Fish were moving everywhere in classic, splashy surface rises. Thinking they were feeding on chironomids, which were hatching abundantly, that's what we used . . . but the fish would have none of it. Near dark we lifted anchor and allowed the breeze to push us the quarter-mile directly back to camp. This method of fishing is called "mooching", but it's really just trolling using natural elements. One of my favourite flies for mooching is a big leech, used with a heavy type III sinking line.

We hadn't moved far when I hooked a bright two pound fish. I release nearly all fish, especially big guys. It's just a personal thing . . . However, the two-pounder would be dinner that night. At camp we examined its stomach and found the fish crammed with water boatmen! It was then we realized the arching-feeding pattern had been there for us to recognize . . . and we hadn't.

Our great expectations were dashed the next morning by a howling wind which had come up overnight. Two of us rowing mightily on one set of oars for a full hour only got our boat half way up the lake. Exhausted, we quartered the waves into a cove to "regroup." Out of direct wind we were able to set the anchors and make a few casts. We took fish, all small, but it was not a comfortable day so by noon we headed back. As we hit shore in front of camp we noticed thousands upon thousands of corixa stacked up in the foam along the shoreline, carried there by the waves. Certainly with that many available, the fish would be gorged anyway.

Alf and I went back to Minnie the following weekend, but the corixa "hatch" was over by then and all we were able to catch were a couple of big dark spawners at the south end. It was the last time either of us fished there . . .

There is a trick when fishing water boatmen patterns which I have found out-produces any other method. Keep in mind that fish almost always hit boatmen as they turn to go back down after capturing their bubble of air. Using a full slow sink line, apply a heavy coating of floatant to the last ten feet of line, all your leader, and the fly. Cast and let the belly of the line sink until it starts to pull the greased portion under, then strip your line in short erratic bursts to imitate the boatmen heading back down to the weeds. Pause once in a while and let the fly drift up towards the surface . . . then "pull" it back down. It can be deadly! But one caution: fish *never* hit this fly softly so resist the temptation to strike back!

Another method, taught to me by my friend Doug Swisher, involves using a pattern tied on a styrofoam body . . . which obviously floats. Doug's corixa has rubber legs to represent the "oars", and fished with a sinking line they really impart live–action as the fly is pulled towards the bottom.

Still another method is to splice–in a ten foot section of floating line at the end of your sinking line . . . Unfortunately, just as you get the hang of fishing water boatman patterns, fish turn to other feed. For some reason these little guys only interest fish for a few days at a time even though they are always in fair abundance.

I should also mention the larger cousins to water boatman: Notonectidae, the backswimmers. These are not as abundant as boatmen and are therefore not always as available to fish.

As their name implies, this insect swims on its back which means the air bubble it carries in its abdominal pocket rides in an "upright" position . . . much like a swimmer in the ocean floating on his back grasping a beachball to his chest.

Physical characteristics of backswimmers are similar to water boatmen except they are larger, reaching a size of about 16mm., and movement is altered by the air bubble. Patterns should have a casing of clear plastic over a light colored body, "oars", and a full–length dark wing casing. Tied properly these will roll over in the water so the plastic rides up with the hook point inverted.

Needless to say there is controversy surrounding this pattern, some advocates saying it doesn't matter how it rides in the water. But master fly fishers with far more knowledge than I, insist it must be fished "properly" to have good success.

In any event, every complete fly box will have patterns representing both corixa and notonecta, so that when you see fish moving along the top in swift head to tail rises, you'll know what to use.

Entomology Profile
Common Name: Water Boatman

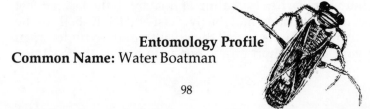

Taxonomic Classification: Order Hemiptera, Family Corixidae

Size Range: 3–11 mm. in length

Colouration: two tone with shellback a dark brown and abdomen a pale yellow. The abdomen appears silvery in appearance as it is enveloped in a bubble of air used for respiration.

Preferred Habitat: Water Boatmen are found in lakes and ponds throughout the world. In the Interior lakes of British Columbia they are common inhabitants of the shallow shoal areas where they feed on detritus and various small invertebrate larvae.

Availability to Trout: Immature and adult boatmen are available year round but are preferred mainly in spring just after ice-off and in the late fall when females dive into the lake to deposit eggs.

Life Cycle: Larva of Water Boatmen go through a series of molts before finally emerging as a winged adult. The adults then mature late in the fall and complete mating away from the water. The females then return to release eggs on submerged vegetation.

It is the returning flight of egg-laden females that stirs the interest of trout. The "egg laying" flight often occurs on bright sunny days in late September. The sight of females diving into the lake often resembles a rain shower. Trout will characteristically follow the flight around the lake.

Distinguishing Features: The hind legs of the Water Boatman are elongated and oar-like in appearance giving rise to their name. They also swim normally versus back-swimmers which swim on their back. Water Boatmen must surface on a regular basis to replenish their air supply.

Entomology Profile

Common Name: Backswimmer

Taxonomic Classification: Order Hemiptera, Family Notonectidae

Size Range: 5–15 mm. in length

Colouration: Back or shell-back shades of tan to yellow while abdomen is generally dark brown or black. As name implies this insect swims on its back. The Backswimmer also traps a bubble of air on its abdomen thus giving it a silvery appearance.

Preferred Habitat: As with Water Boatmen, the Backswimmer has worldwide distribution. They are present in most small lakes and ponds in British Columbia and typically inhabit shallow shoal areas. They are predators feeding on other aquatic invertebrates and even small fish.

Availability to Trout: Year round although most sought after during spring and fall "egg laying" flights

Life Cycle: Development of Backswimmers is similar to Water Boatmen as the larvae develop through a series of molts. The winged adults are capable of mating twice a year in the spring and late fall. "Nuptual" flights occur as the adults leave the lake to mate. The females return soon after diving into the lake to attach her eggs on submerged vegetation. The "egg laying" flights are actively followed by trout.

Distinguishing Features: Backswimmers are the only aquatic invertebrate that swims on its back. Backswimmers also attain a greater size than Water Boatmen. These insects must surface on a regular basis to replenish their air supply.

XIII
Leech: The Undulator

by Alf Davy

Have you ever fly cast with aquatic worms? In my earlier years of fly fishing, I had heard that a leech pattern was a good fly to use. The first impression that came to my mind was a long, dark undulating body of three to five inches in length. But nowhere in my fly box was a fly that large.

To compound the problem was the fact that there were very few commercial leech patterns. I could have used a Doc Spratley, Carey Special, or Woolly Worm in dark colours to try and imitate a leech. I tried some with dark wool and others with peacock herl tied Carey–style. They took fish but I was never sure the fish were taking them as a leech.

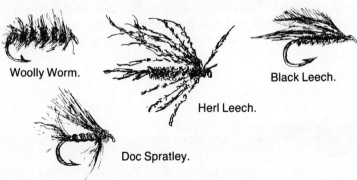

Woolly Worm.

Black Leech.

Herl Leech.

Doc Spratley.

For many years, I never found a leech in the stomach contents of any fish that I cleaned. I kept thinking of those long, dark, undulating shapes that I saw swimming in the water. I was doubtful that a fish would be able to eat them, let alone want them. The question I kept asking myself was how a three-quarter pound fish could ever get something that size completely in its mouth.

The result of all this conjecture was that I was very skeptical about leech stories and leech flies. I certainly did not fish them with any confidence and they were always the last patterns I would turn to.

However, as I came into contact with more skilled fly fishermen, I got to know some truths about leeches. First, the ones that fish eat are the young, small ones about one to one-and-a-half inches in length. Second, fish take them near or on the bottom. Third, leech patterns seemed to be most effective in the evening, and last, the smaller fish do not seem to feed on them to the same degree larger fish do. Once I had established these facts, I started to catch the odd fish on leech patterns. It was then a matter of working on the patterns to make them more reliable and efficient.

My first lesson came in a lake near Kamloops one evening when I fished with a couple of friends that were proficient with leech patterns. They would go out in the late evenings to shoal areas and watch for cruising or feeding fish. When fish were spotted they would cast, with sinking line and weighted fly, far enough ahead of the fish to allow the fly to sink to the bottom. If the fish arrived at the spot where the fly was sitting they would twitch and move it to attract the fish. If they were casting in deeper water and in a random pattern, they used a weighted leech that had the front third of the hook bent and the weight added there. This weight distribution allowed the fly to be retrieved with an undulating movement as it was alternately moved forward then allowed to rest and drop. The weighted front half would dip down and sink first, then it would rise up as the line was retrieved. I had now learned two ways to fish leeches — in the shallows and in mid-water.

Bent Hook Leech.

Another method of fishing the leech came by chance as I

was fishing a dragon nymph in a deep drop-area one early summer day. I caught a large fish whose stomach was filled with leeches of about one inch in length. I had been fishing slowly on the bottom with the dragon when the fish had taken. I was now determined to tie up a leech pattern that I could use when fish were eating small leeches near the lake bottom.

I figured that the pattern I wanted should be one that could be fished slowly on the bottom or slightly faster in mid-water. I came up with a fly that had a black seal hair body, marabou tail and hackle for a life-like movement. The first time I tried this pattern I had fantastic success. Large fish would violently strike this leech pattern while it slowly moved along the bottom. I always have a selection of various colours and sizes in my fly box but I have found that black and maroon are best. I like to use extra-long hooks in sizes six to ten.

Marabou is the best material I have found to give leech patterns a live-like action in the water. I use marabou that range in colour from black to grey, dark to light green, and dark brown to tan, and mottled in any of these colours. I tie the tail of marabou material to a length never longer than the length of the hook shank. The body of the fly is clipped deer hair dubbed over with black seal. I tie the odd clump of marabou along the shank and one last clump at the eye of the hook. This fly became known as the "All Black" during my year of using it in New Zealand. Another way is to tie in clumps of dark acrylic yarn and then brush it with a hair brush to give it a uniform look.

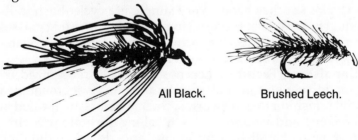

All Black.   Brushed Leech.

The way I fish this leech pattern is to move it slowly on the bottom with a slow inch by inch hand weave retrieve. When fishing mid-water I use longer pulls of 6 to 12 inches. If you are fishing mid-water, you will experience a lot of short hits. You must learn not to strike at the short hits but to continue your retrieve. The fish will come back at the fly from the side or front with a more violent strike.

I now look forward to summer and fall days when I know larger fish will be feeding on leeches. I find that this is the best time to use a good leech pattern. It is also one of my best patterns for evening fish. I now have good success with leech patterns because I fish them with confidence and knowledge.

Fish Food Profile

Common Name: Leech

Taxonomic Classification: Class Hirudinea

Size Range: When fully extended (swimming) may reach up to 150 mm. in length. Common sizes generally less than 80 mm.

Colouration: Solid and mottled variations of black, brown and maroon.

Preferred Habitat: Leeches are found in almost all shallow interior lakes but are perhaps more abundant in the dark water lily pad types. Leeches prey on insect larvae, snails and shrimp but are also scavengers feeding on dead or decaying organic matter. They are capable of swimming but spend most of their time in the bottom (benthic) areas of the lake where they find both food and shelter. It is suggested they are more active nocturnally using the cover of darkness to swim around in search of food or shelter areas. However, there are occasions when leeches are observed swimming in open water areas during daylight hours. During these periods they are extremely vulnerable to predation.

Availability to Trout: Year round but more sought after during warmest water conditions.

Life Cycle: Leeches have a very simple life cycle. Each individual is capable of reproducing by itself. Once egg masses are produced, the leech attaches them to some underwater object thus starting a new generation.

Distinguishing Features: Leeches are easily recognized by their dorso-ventrally flattened body which is segmented in similar fashion to earthworms. Sucking discs are located at either end and are used to "inch" along the bottom. Swimming is accomplished by an up and down undulating motion of the body.

XIV
Brookies: Fish of the Shallow Lakes

by Brian Chan

Black Lake is one of those small, productive, interior lakes that has all of the ingredients to grow fish. It is 25 kilometres southeast of Kamloops, B.C., and just a stone's throw from popular Roche Lake. Contrary to its name, the waters of Black Lake are a clear aqua green color and look very attractive to the flyfisherman. Numerous small bays, gentle drop-offs, and an inviting weed–covered, sunken island offer ideal habitat for the Brook trout that reside there.

It was in late July that I first fished this lake and had my first encounter with this member of the char family. That day the only other person catching fish was an older gentleman who, now that I think back, was an experienced Brookie fisherman. He would cast a large fly on a sinking line, strip–off the remaining flyline and a considerable amount of back–ing and then begin rowing. He directed the boat parallel to, but just off the drop off so the fly was fishing very close to the bottom. The unique part of his technique was that every 4 or 5 strokes of the oars, he would pick up the rod and give it several quick jerks. Invariably, as he would place the rod down, the fish would hit. I watched his technique long enough to decide that these fish could also be caught on a cast fly. Anchoring in 20 feet of water, just off the sunken island, I put on a high–density sinking line and a large black leech pattern. The first few casts helped to determine when to begin retrieving the fly so that it fished as close to the bottom as possible. After collecting several feet of line, using a hand twist retrieve, I gave the fly 4 or 5 quick pulls. Just as I was beginning a slow hand twist again, I had a strike that was hard enough to break-off cleanly. I increased the leader tippet to 6 lb., tied on another leech and cast out again. On the third set of quick pulls, I hit another fish. Its fight reminded me of spring salmon on the coast, sounding deep and twisting violently, trying to shake the hook. Fish that day weighed between 1½ and 4 pounds. Ten years later, I still use this technique with consistent results.

Leech.

Eastern Brook trout or Brook trout, as they are commonly known as, have limited distribution in B.C. and are confined mainly to the southern portion of the province. These members of the char family are not native to B.C., but were originally brought into the province in 1908 when 35,000 eggs from Quebec were placed in the Fraser Valley Hatchery at Abbotsford. This transfer was the first attempt to establish Brook trout anywhere in Canada outside of its native range.

From the original liberations in B.C. waters, the provincial hatchery system has been able to culture "naturalized stocks". At present, up to 1.2 million Brook trout are released annually into lakes, predominantly in the Williams Lake, Kamloops, and Okanagan areas.

Brookies are most valuable to the fisheries manager because of their ability to withstand much harsher environmental conditions than that of Rainbow trout. They are often selected for stocking into "marginal" lakes that potentially winter or summer kill. The char are able to survive the lower oxygen conditions associated with these lakes during certain periods of the year. The productive nature of these marginal lakes is often reflected in the tremendous growth rates of the stocked Brook trout. Released in May, as 6 month-old fry, these char can grow to a very chunky 8 to 11 inch fish by the fall of the same year! Under prolonged favourable conditions, they are able to attain weights in excess of 8 pounds. Size is often deceiving as these fish tend to be very deep-bodied and short in overall length.

The freshwater shrimp *Gammarus* is the staple food of most Brook trout populations in interior lakes. These shrimp are prolific breeders and are generally very abundant. A regular diet of shrimp is responsible for the deep orange flesh colour of both Brook and Rainbow trout. Other important food sources include chironomids, damsel and dragonflies, mayflies, caddisflies, backswimmers, waterboatmen and

Shrimp.

leeches. Some situations occur where coarse fish (shiners, chub) coexist with Brook trout. These minnows often become an important food item as the Brookies attain larger sizes.

Char species in general are noted as being opportunistic feeders. Perhaps this best explains how on one occasion I found a large field mouse "intact" in the stomach of a 3 pound fish!

Hatches of chironomids, mayflies and the mating flights of waterboatman are favoured food items from ice-off to early summer. As the lake water continues to warm-up, the Brook trout begin feeding on emerging caddisflies, damselflies, and dragonflies.

By mid-summer, Brookies are seeking out the cooler depths of the lake. Anglers must be prepared to fish sinking lines and use such techniques as described earlier in the chapter. I also believe Brook trout are a schooling fish, especially during the warm summer period. If fishing slows down in a particular spot, one should be prepared to move around rather than wait for the fish to possibly return. Shoreline features such as large rocky drop-offs are preferred habitat. I have often observed fish cruising back and forth along rocky areas then suddenly darting into the rocks to pick up either dragonfly nymphs, leeches or shrimp.

As with Rainbow fishing, one should pay close attention to the insect activity occuring on the lake. Brook trout definitely feed on the "hatches", but possibly not to the same degree of exclusiveness that Rainbows are known for. For instance, a good Callibaetis mayfly hatch will certainly promote feeding activity but a large dragonfly nymph fished through a feeding area would almost assuredly attract some attention.

Earlier chapters in this book have described in detail various fishing techniques for the different trout foods. These methods apply directly to Brook trout fishing as well.

Brook trout and the other members of the char family differ physiologically from Rainbow trout in that they are fall rather than spring spawners. By early September, the maturing male brookies have developed a brilliant crimson red colouration along the lower portion of the body. This is offset by very distinct white-coloured leading edges of pectoral and pelvic fins. A well-developed hooked nose or kipe completes the appearance of the mature male. Gravid females show increased colouration of body spots to an almost orange-red color, as well as developing the white tipped body fins. The mature fish begin cruising along the lake shoreline in search of a suitable spawning stream. Most lakes are landlocked or have minimal stream flows by fall. It is therefore common to see these fish attempting to "shore spawn" in spring-fed gravel or rubble patches in the shallow water zone. Successful hatching of eggs from this type of spawning is often limited but the major benefit is the opportunity for these mature fish to "clean up" and begin actively feeding again. It is interesting to note that the spawning cycle is physically much less demanding on Brook trout than on Rainbow trout.

Brookies offer an exciting alternative to Rainbow fishing particularly during the warm summer months. While the Rainbow become very selective and sometimes difficult to catch, the Brook trout will continue to feed and offer challenging angling opportunities.

XV
Steelhead on
the Wet Fly

by Ehor Boyanowsky

For me, nothing compares with the thrill of a 20 lb. Thompson River steelhead rising from the depths of a pool to slash at my high–floating dry fly. But I must confess, every time I convinced myself I had the formula for dry fly success all worked out, some bushy–tailed upstart using a subsurface fly would reduce my confidence to a mass of self–doubt.

What I have come to realize is that in steelheading, *presentation* of the fly is of paramount importance while the flies themselves are a minor factor, perhaps only two percent. I don't mean to denegrate the importance of flies — surely the pattern may sometimes spell the difference between getting that sulky old hook jaw to rise just once more or ignore the offering entirely. Rather, in the manner peculiar to devotees of any religion (which steelheading surely is), we spend 98 percent of our time discussing and pondering that (contro-versial) two percent, and then present the fly in a manner that we most enjoy for esthetic reasons. The procedure I believe in, then, is the premise that we should fly fish for steelhead for the beauty of the experience.

The full measure of the steelhead experience is achieved when we present a fly — perhaps one we pondered and created — to a specific fish we can see holding in the depths of the pool, watch the fish rise to take the fly, and then feel to the most sensuous degree possible, its primal struggle, savouring it through to escape or release. And occasionally, if we so choose, we may take the fish as bounty for the table. It is only on rare occasion that the total experience is fulfilled in all the parameters of skill and emotion we seek, but we should none-the-less strive towards those ideals.

Floating Line Wet Fly

I have found on several rivers including the Thompson, Dean and Campbell that a wet fly fished just subsurface will provoke a take. When one is using a floating line there are a number of ways to achieve shallow depth fly presentation. The simplest way is to use a leader of 9 to 12 feet with a tippet strength calculated to turn over the size of fly used. In the waters of British Columbia, flies sized 2, 4 and 6 are the most popular. These flies require a tippet strength of 8 to 12 pounds to turn them over properly. My rule of thumb is to use the strongest tippet size that conditions will allow in order to bring the fish under control and to beach it without undue stress caused by having to play it too gingerly.

Occasionally, I will fish for "half-pounders" (summer steelhead of one to four pounds that migrate up coastal streams for short periods of time) and in that situation, a reduction in size of fly and tippet is in order. Small flies, especially those tied in low water style, can prove more effective on these fish.

When using a floating line, cast the fly directly across the stream and as it touches down, 'mend' the line with an upstream flick of the rod. This upstream belly provides some slack in the line between fly and rod so that, as the fly begins its swing, it is allowed to sink a few inches before the line, with its greater resistance, catches up, putting the fly under tension and accelerating its speed. To sink the fly deeper, cast upstream rather than across and flick coiled slack line upstream in a technique called "spaghetti mending". The fly will spend more time drifting without tension and large flies, dressed low water style ($1/0$, $2/0$, $3/0$) will sink even deeper. When presenting in clear water to specific fish, this is the counterpart of the nymph presentation, or the "patent method" as it is known in Atlantic Salmon circles. Of course fishing upstream presenting the fly dead drift and deeply sunk, you no longer cover the wider area involved in a downstream sweep. Thus the method lends itself best to fishing narrow rivers where exact lies are known.

Because this method requires maximum line control it has repopularized the double taper line that requires more false casting and does not shoot as well but makes mending a pleasure. Weight forward lines are generally preferred for distance casting. Floating, shooting heads are even more efficient but are not as pleasurable to cast (and are almost impossible to mend precisely).

A new, very expensive braided leader from West Germany that allegedly sinks very efficiently will extend the conditions under which the floating line can be used. Of course, even two tiny split shots just above the tippet can also be used to sink leaders without too severely impeding casting ability.

Sinking Lines

I feel a much more pleasurable alternative to split shot is to use a wet tip, sink tip, or wet belly line. These designations have in common the characteristic that some length of the line's tip, depending on its density, will sink the fly anywhere from a few inches below the surface to a point where one is bottom-bouncing. Unfortunately, a high density tip on a fly line can make it ungainly to cast, sometimes producing a hinging effect that is especially troublesome for beginners and irritating for good fly casters. The ridiculous extreme involves attaching 4 to 5 feet of lead core to a floating line. It can be very dangerous to the angler and casts with all the delicacy of a downrigger, but can be deadly for fly fishers needing to hook fish at all costs, "on the fly". To overcome this problem, California fly casters years ago developed the shooting head system of a monofilament running line, or #2 floating level fly line of considerable length, to which is attached shooting heads of 20–40 feet of various densities ranging from slow sinking to lead core. These outfits will cast a mile and, if looped rather than spliced to the running line, can be changed quickly. They are extremely effective on large streams but require a "whip" type of casting not enjoyed by some and not easily controlled by mending. In addition, especially on narrower streams, such a considerable length of sinking line can become wrapped around rocks and stumps and consequently lost. At $20 a head, this can be a costly exercise. Clearly then, attempts to sink a fly right to the bottom involve a compromise between grace, casting ease and efficiency.

Finally, one last point to be made involves leader length. I have watched numerous anglers go to all kinds of extremes to get their lines to sink then counter-productively attach 9 foot leaders!

As Lefty Kreh has shown, with a sinking line, leader length is not important to avoid spooking the fish. However, I have found a leader length of 4 to 6 feet makes casting more pleasant and keeps an unweighted fly swimming slightly above the lower depth of the line itself. Thus, the first thing to touch a rock or the bottom will be the line which is more likely to remain unsnagged. After all, fish do not literally lie on the stream bed itself, but are suspended at least a foot or two above. Summer run fish (those entering the river, anywhere from 6 to 12 months before they spawn) will usually take a fly sunk anywhere from the surface film to a couple of feet below. One need not pass the fly before their noses unless the water is turbid, extremely high in temperature (above 62°F) or the fish are close to spawning. They are less affected by cold water temperatures than winter run fish. For the winter run fish, a fly is most effectively presented in front of their noses unless there is a sudden rise in temperature as on a bright, sunny day in March or April. Theories of fly presentation that deal only with water temperature are like all theories; in part correct but, I believe, miss the most important distinction — genetic make up of the fish.

The Wet Fly

And now for the controversial two percent. There are, perhaps, as many theories regarding fly effectiveness as there are flies. Certainly I have never come upon an Atlantic salmon stream without the gilly telling me that none of the flies in my box was any good. This past summer in Scotland was no exception, and when I sneaked a Miramichi Bomber onto my line and fished it unorthodoxically on a wet–tip, my gilly was astonished. When after two days, it had accounted for all of our fish, he became a convert.

For all of my steelhead fishing, I favour only three basic patterns. One of them, the Thompson River Rat derived from the Miramichi Bomber, a torpedo shape of spun caribou hair, is usually fished dry. In wet fly fishing the remaining two categories are *bright*, ranging from day glow orange to hot pink and golden yellow, and *dark*, meaning basically black with heads, tips or hackle of bright red, orange or green. I find the bright flies, whether impressionistic attractors such as the General Practitioner, my own Davie Street Hooker or Joe Kambeitz's prawn–imitating Squamish Poacher work best sunk deep in cold, clear water for winter runs. I find dark flies work best for summer runs fished from the surface film in clear water to deep sunk in turbid water. My own favourite is the MacLeod — a slim, black, green butt, bear hair winged fly. Dark flies, rather than bright flies, are most easily seen in low light conditions or turbid waters. Under those conditions, Art Lingren's tie of the Black Practitioner has worked well, and that, of course, also explains why the Miramichi Bomber with its heavy dark profile and active body hair worked well in the peat-stained waters of Scotland for Atlantic salmon.

Optimum size of fly and thickness of profile are largely dictated by water volume which is determined either by size of the river or its water level. Use a small fly in small rivers unless the river is high, in which case the size should be increased accordingly. Similarly, reduce the size of fly even on a large river when water is low and clear and fish are pool-bound and spooky. Although some may argue that steelhead are not spooky, a fear reaction to sighting an angler or predator need not be marked by a flurry of activity. The fish may subtly change orientation so that its nose is pointing more to the streambed and less toward a preferred lie, or it can move behind, rather than in front of, a rock (the ideal taking position).

I suspect the reason for this preference to protect its head and forward body is that, if grabbed towards the tail it is more likely to escape if its head is clear. Thus, a fish holding with its head exposed is an aggressive, taking fish, or at least one that has not been spooked.

Remember, because a steelhead is usually much larger than most resident trout, you do not have to set the hook on the take. Give it time to turn away so the hook point can imbed itself in the hinge of the jaw. Then firmly tighten up and thrill to the sweet song of the reel!

XVI
Summer Steelhead on the Dry Fly

by Mike Maxwell

Every angler must dream of fishing his favourite stream and watching spellbound as a large steelhead rises to his carefully controlled dryfly and finally swallows it with a huge swirl. This dream can come true providing the angler has the patience to learn a few basic facts about the habits and life-cycle of steelhead, has the basic ability to make the correct fly presentation and has the discipline to carefully cover all the water thoroughly. The special method of finding, hooking, playing and releasing a large fish on dryfly is easily learned.

In my opinion, what makes steelheading so fascinating is that unlike resident feeding trout, migrating steelhead in many cases are not feeding and are dominated by the urge to reach their spawning beds. The big puzzle is, why do they take a dryfly? In an attempt to explain this phenomenon, it is useful to examine the life-cycle of the fish and its food during its juvenile period and its behaviour during its upstream migration.

Steelhead are spawned and spend their juvenile years in the upper reaches of the river and during this period they feed on many forms of underwater insect life. To escape the underwater and aerial predators, they keep close to any safe hiding place that is near or contains food and has good clean oxygenated water. In steelhead streams the juvenile fish's habitat is usually under large rocks or in and around beds of very large gravel that are sheltered from the fast current. By a happy coincidence of nature, a large stonefly nymph has exactly the same habitat as the juvenile steelhead and forms a major portion of its diet. This relationship of large gravel, stonefly nymphs and juvenile steelhead is extremely important when locating the resting or holding stations of the upward migrating mature steelhead, and can be called "juvenile habitat imprint".

Although the underwater nymph is significant, it is the effect of the flying adult stonefly on the juvenile fish that is important to the dryfly angler. The stonefly nymph completes its lifecycle by crawling out of the water onto the beach, drying itself, slitting its nymph case and emerging as a very large stonefly adult. After mating, the female deposits her eggs by fluttering down and dipping her egg sack into the water. This process is repeated many times and is so clumsy that it causes a large disturbance above and on the water. The curious thing about stoneflies is that they do not swarm and cause feeding periods as mayfly or caddis do and can often be seen singly or in small groups. During its juvenile period and stream migration, the immature steelhead must compete for food with many other fish. One fluttering stonefly has the food value of a dozen caddis or mayflies and its appearance will trigger an immediate competitive feeding response from many juvenile fish, some of them not much bigger than the fly. It is this relationship of the appearance of a single fly and the immediate triggered response of the juvenile fish that is important in understanding why an upward migrating, non-feeding fish will take a dryfly. This behaviour can be called "the single fly juvenile feeding imprint". It is important to note that in most cases the natural adult stoneflies have completed their egg laying cycle and are not present during the steelhead stream migration. Adult stonefly activity is usually over by the middle of summer.

It must always be remembered that the natural habitat of the steelhead is the ocean and that it uses the river as an incubator and nursery only and will return to the sea after spawning. The juvenile fish will also go to sea to feed and mature, when it is strong enough to withstand the rigours of the journey.

Very little is known about the ocean life of steelhead; however, one important fact is that they do not school and will return to their river singly when sexually mature. Even though many fish may enter the river together, congregating or pairing does not usually take place until reaching the spawning beds. The timing of the upward migration of summer steelhead will vary for each river, though it will usually occur between early summer and late fall on the more productive rivers.

The rate of travel of an upward migrating fish will depend on the rate of flow of the river, natural obstacles and its ability to detect the chemical 'scent' of its parent river. Under favourable conditions, fish can travel many miles a day and must stop to rest occasionally. Once it becomes known that summer steelhead are in the river, it is relatively easy to locate them. Remember that they are using the steam as a highway and looking for a rest area free of current and with easy access and return to the stream. Rest areas can be at any point in a river, such as behind large rocks or close to the bank in shallow water. In long shallow pools, they will nearly always hold adjacent to the very large gravel similar to their habitat as juveniles. This is "the juvenile habitat imprint" mentioned earlier and is the most productive location on many rivers. Discarded stonefly nymph shucks or skins will usually confirm that you are in the right place. It is sometimes possible to see holding fish rising to caddis, even though they are not actually feeding. Fish that can be seen rolling in fast, deep water are usually moving through, and many hours can be wasted fishing to a fish that is no longer there.

Having located a holding area, it is possible to present an artificial adult stonefly in such a way as to trigger the fishes "single fly juvenile feeding imprint". This is accomplished by imitating the clumsy movements of the female stonefly as she deposits her eggs in the water. The line is cast out, across stream, directly upstream from the hold. As the fly starts to swing in, the line is mended upstream and additional line is fed through the guides. This process is repeated, causing the visible dry fly to jerk and bubble straight downstream. It is this action that fools the fish and triggers his "juvenile feeding imprint". At the end of the controlled drift, the fly is allowed to swing in towards shore and this movement will also trigger strikes as it imitates a stonefly being blown across the water. Before casting again, the line is stripped in to the original cast length and the process is repeated. Don't worry about sloppy casts or rough mends as they usually produce the fly movement we are trying to achieve.

It can be seen from the diagram that this presentation covers a lot of water and that the fly is fished both on the drift,

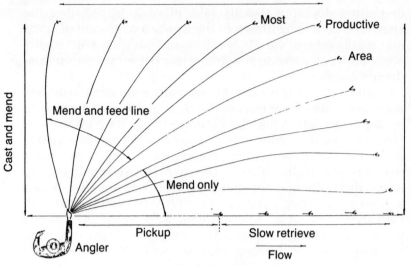

Feed and Mend Presentation

Controlled drift

Cast and mend

Most ⟶ ⸲ Productive

⸲ Area

Mend and feed line

Mend only

Pickup

Slow retrieve

Angler

Flow

River Bank

on the swing and also on the retrieve and not just on the swing as is traditional in steelheading.

As the fly passes near an interested fish, it will usually leave its hold and drift down the river behind the fly and make a close inspection. This process may have to be repeated many times before a take occurs. In most cases, you will actually see the fish and sometimes you can watch as the fly is taken into an open mouth. This is what makes dryfly steelhead so heart-stopping as it all happens right up on the surface in front of you.

When the fish has raised and come to the fly you must "feed the fly to the fish" and make it hook itself. Many anglers do not understand this process and consequently lose many fish by pulling the fly out of the fish's mouth before it is hooked properly. I believe that as steelhead are not feeding, they do not close their mouths tight on a fly and any attempt to strike will mean a lost fish. To further complicate matters, any tension on the line will tell the fish that the fly is not a natural and it will reject it. If the fish can take the fly without feeling any connection to the line, it will turn and swim upstream back to its hold, pulling the fly into the corner of its jaw. This location of hook is almost impossible to pull out and, providing your leader knots hold, you should land your fish. Lip-hooked fish will usually throw the fly or straighten it. Feeding the fly to the fish is accomplished as follows: At all times during the presentation, the rod is held as vertical as possible, so as to create as much slack in the line as possible and give the fish the impression that the fly is not connected to anything. There is usually enough slack during the drift stage. However, if a fish comes to the fly on the across stream swing, the rod is lowered, giving even more slack. At no time during the entire process is it necessary to strike.

Having hooked the fish, the next stage is to land and release it. Dryfly hooks are usually made with light wire and they can break if too much pressure is put on the fish. If common sense is used and the angler does not panic then huge fish can be landed on small flies.

There are a few basic rules to follow which are illustrated by the following: If an angler is standing upstream and is holding the rod high this has the effect of lifting the fish out of the water and pulling it upstream and does very little to bring the fish to the bank. But when the angler has moved directly across stream from the fish and lowered the bent rod close to the surface, he is producing the "maximum effective lateral force" (or using the current to bring fish in and not pulling the fish against the current). Remember, if your intention is to bring the fish to the river bank, you should not be trying to lift it out of the water or pull it upstream. The across stream landing technique usually causes the fish to stay close to its hold as it does not feel any life threatening pull from upstream or downstream. This is useful when working on a fish close to rapids. The rod tip may have to be raised occasionally, so that the leader does not drag on obstacles such as rocks.

This easy and logical method will enable you to land a fish quickly so that it can be released with the maximum chance of survival. Play the fish, but do not "play with it". The sooner you land it, the sooner you can be fishing again.

When releasing a fish, keep it in the water and use pliers to remove the fly. Do not drag it onto the beach and let it beat itself to death on the rocks. If the fly is difficult to remove, just cut the leader and leave the fly in, as the natural acids in the fish will soon rust out a light dryfly. Before releasing the fish, make sure that it has recovered enough to swim in the current you are releasing it in. It is possible to determine the weight of a fish by measuring its length and girth. (It is good practice to have someone else do this, as fish seem to get bigger when the angler does the measuring.) Carry a tape and measure the length of the fish between the nose and the fork in the tail. It is a curious fact that estimated lengths and weights tend to make the fish larger than it really is!

Successful summer steelheading depends to a large extent on a careful study of the river and formulating a "game

119

plan" before even entering the water. The following procedure should be adequate for most rivers.

1. "Read the water" and decide on the length of pool to be fished.
2. Note potential holding areas and obvious rocks.
3. Move to the head of the pool and wade out ankle deep.
4. Carry out the cast, "feed and mend" and drift, starting with a 30 ft. cast. Repeat this three times.
5. Repeat this process with 40 ft.–50 ft. and 60 ft. casts.
6. Reel in and move downstream 15 ft. and repeat. Remember to stay ankle deep only.
7. When the end of the pool is reached, return to the starting point, wade out to your crotch and repeat the whole process.
8. Concentrate on any visible rocks or rising fish, but don't forget to fish the other water.
9. Don't fall into the trap of thinking that the fish are only on the other side of the river. To have someone hook a fish behind you while you are trying to cast to the other side is humiliating.

The following is a short list of equipment needed for dryfly steelheading:

1. Felt soled chest waders: (metal "cleats" if the rocks are very slippery)
2. As long a rod as possible for ease of mending the line.
3. A #7 or #8 double taper or long belly floating line.
4. A reel with 100 yd. of 30 lb. backing and rim control drag.
5. A 10 ft. leader with a heavy butt section.
6. Polaroid sunglasses.
7. Measuring tape.
8. Needle nose pliers.
9. Fly flotant.

The fly used will vary in size according to the size of the natural and will vary between #10 and #4. The style of fly must be such that the body will float low in the water and have a high wing that will still be visible to the angler at long distances. It should closely match the color and shape of the natural of that area.

Dryfly steelheading has made many converts over the last few years and is a natural step in the evolution of a flyfisher. It is now no longer necessary to stand in water up to your armpits mindlessly casting out flies that resemble Christmas tree ornaments. To induce a non–feeding, migratory fish to take a dryfly by triggering its basic juvenile feeding habits is fishing at its highest form and is about as close to nature as an angler can get.

Entomology Profile
Common Name: Stonefly nymph and adult
Taxonomic Classification: Order Plecoptera

Size Range: Nymphs and adults may range in length from 5 to 50 mm. excluding antennae and tails.

Colouration: Dependant on species and habitat, nymphs and adults come in various shades of yellow, orange, brown and black. Often they appear two tone, such as black dorsally and yellow-orange on the underside.

Preferred Habitat: The many thousands of kilometres of rivers and streams found throughout B.C. provides ample habitat for a wide diversity of stonefly species. The insects are an important food item to almost all salmonids inhabiting these moving waters.

Stoneflies are known as biological indicators of water quality because of their requirement of highly oxygenated water for respiration. As such, most nymphs are found in rivers and streams, although a few families are capable of living along exposed rocky shoal areas of cold water lakes.

The nymphs inhabit the stream bottom areas of the water course seeking cover under debris piles, fallen trees and most commonly under rocks.

They are considered sluggish swimmers and prefer to crawl around in search of food. Some species are carnivorous, preying on mayfly nymphs and dipteran larvae while others are strictly herbivorous utilizing algae and vegetative detritus. As nymphs develop and food sources change numerous stonefly families will ''drift'' downstream in search of better habitat conditions.

Availability to Trout: As nymphs year round but possibly selected more as fully developed nymphs crawl towards shore for emergence into adult. As adults the egg laying females are actively sought after.

Life Cycle: Stoneflies exhibit an incomplete metamorphosis as the adult emerges directly from the nymph. Dependent on species the nymphs require from 6 months to 3 years and as many as 25 instars or molts to develop completely. Stoneflies are capable of emerging at all times of the year but emergence is dependent on species and appropriate water temperatures. Fully developed nymphs crawl to shore and climb out of the water to complete transformation. As the nymph dries off a dorsal split develops in the exoskeleton (or skin) and the adult crawls out. The fully formed adult then crawls or flies away. Most adult species are active during the dawn and dusk periods. Through the daylight hours they seek refuge in vegetation or under streambank rocks.

Mating occurs on land usually in nearby trees. Mated females return to the water to deposit eggs. Dispersal of eggs is accomplished in several ways. Most females fly low over the water touching the tip of the abdomen to the surface and releasing eggs. Some species release eggs while hovering over the water, yet others crawl into the water and attach eggs to submerged objects. The adult portion of the stonefly life cycle may last up to several weeks.

Distinguishing Features: Stonefly nymphs are recognized by their somewhat flattened slender body, distinct wing pads and widely separated eyes. They also possess long slender antennae and two tails. Gill filaments, often brightly coloured, are present on the throat, bases of legs and abdomen. Nymphs are generally poor swimmers and thus have developed claws at the ends of their legs for crawling mobility in strong currents. Stonefly and mayfly nymphs can be distinguished from each other by the presence or absence of antennae.

Adults have elongated wings which are held flat over the body and extend past the tip of the abdomen. They also possess a pair of slender antennae and two relatively short tails.

Stonefly Nymph.

XVII
Salt Water Salmon on the Fly
by Barry Thornton

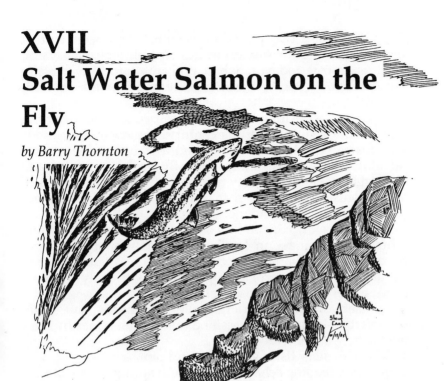

One pursuit which has both intrigued and perplexed flyfishers in British Columbia since early this century, is fly casting to salmon in open salt water.

The earliest writing I have seen with actual reference to this is in the book, *Sunset Playgrounds*, by F. G. Aflalo published in 1909. In a chapter on British Columbia the author says:

"It is needless to add that these Pacific Salmon will not take the fly . . . Various ingenious reasons have been assigned for their reluctance to behave like self-respecting salmon on the Atlantic side, but the real explanation is perfectly simple. It lies in no peculiarity of the salmon themselves, beyond perhaps their reluctance to fool with feather and tinsel when they have so immense a journey before them . . ." ". . . I am indebted to Mr. Cambie . . . the undoubted fact of salmon having occasionally, though not often, been taken on the fly off the mouth of the Fraser, in the clearer salt water."

A decade later, in 1919, ex-provincial game warden, A. Bryan Williams, in his book, *Rod and Creel in British Columbia*, wrote a short chapter entitled, "Fly Fishing For Salmon." In it he stated:

"There were, however, a few men who always used a fly and others who occasionally did, but it has never been followed up as it should, though it is a pretty well acknowledged fact that the cohoe salmon will take the fly freely and the spring salmon occasionally, if it is presented to them properly."

Since these two publications, much has been written about fly fishing for salmon in British Columbia salt water. But it is as true today as when Williams said it over half a century ago, ''. . . it has never been followed up as it should!''

Salmon fly fishing today offers the same challenges that it did at the beginning of the century. However, new tackle and boat access have now reached a standard that makes catching salmon consistently on the fly feasible. Still, I would suggest that, like the mighty river trophy trout, the steelhead, takes at least two years of searching, practice, and experience before an angler's confidence is assured.

Clear water, constantly changing tides, migration patterns, daily changes in feeding patterns, variable weather conditions, and changing feed all contribute in a major way to further the challenge of taking salmon with a fly on open ocean waters. But, it is possible!

Based on my experience over the years, salt water salmon flyfishing can be classified into six categories by locations where salmon are found:

1. Beach–estuary fishing for coho and pinks.
2. Actively feeding schools of coho and springs.
3. Migration points of land.
4. Kelp beds.
5. Shallow feed fish areas.
6. Bluebacks (both coho and pinks) in open waters.

A seasonable classification, when it is possible to consistently catch salmon, would be as follows:

Spring:
*feeding spring schools
*bluebacks and pinks

Summer:
*feeding coho and spring schools
*kelp beds
*shallow feed fish areas
*migrating points of land
*estuary and beach areas for pinks

Fall:
*feeding coho schools
*beach and estuary areas for coho

For the flyfisher first embarking on the challenge of salmon to the fly in salt water, a discussion on tackle is very important in preparation for a day on the water.

The fly rod should be 9' for large fish, a minimum #8, and preferrable a #9 or #10. Fly lines will naturally match the rod and the angler should have a fast sink tip, a full fast sinking line, a shallow wet line, and a floating line. Different fly lines are necessary for each set of conditions encountered but these become the angler's preference as he gains experience.

A good combination system for most situations would be a #8 nine foot rod with a matching #8 weight forward fast sink tip fly line. The fly reel must be one that is anodized or made for salt water use. It should carry at least three hundred yards of backing, and even then, when a large fish is hooked, the boat may have to be used to chase the fish. Leaders must be long and strong. For all salmon except bluebacks, I recommend a minimum 10# test leader of at least 4 to 6 meters. For bluebacks I often go as low as 4# test. And fly hooks must be absolutely sticky–sharp!

In summer, choices of areas to fish from Vancouver Island are many providing weather and fish cooperate. The area I suggest to begin lies off the south end of Quadra Island opposite Campbell River. Runs of migrating coho often hold off the flats at the outer kelp beds, feeding on large schools of herring that feed and seek shelter there. It is the habit of these coho to feed heavily on the morning ebbtide. What we search for on the flats are concentrations of coho feeding near the surface.

This can be the most exciting of all open water salmon fly fishing! Salmon at this time are in a feeding frenzy and they are moving rapidly from area to area seeking herring upon which to feed. This is a chase–and–cast method which demands a good boat and one at which the anglers in the boat must take turns.

Prior to reaching the fishing flats all items should be cleared from the floor of the boat and carefully stowed so that no edges, protruding points, or small items are there to tangle the fly line. Flies are tied to the leader and at least thirty feet of line should be stripped from the reels and coiled either in the angler's hand or on the floor of the boat. In this form of angling, two anglers per boat are a maximum with each taking turns driving the boat and casting to a feeding school of coho.

While travelling through the feeding area, watch for the feeding gulls which will circle above a herring school and then dive down when the coho have chased the herring to the surface. When the driver of the boat sees a flock of gulls suddenly dive to the surface, he should drive the boat immediately to that area, stopping just outside the surfacing herring in position to allow the casting angler a chance to put his fly in the center of the thrashing, feeding coho. The fly is usually an imitation herring fry pattern quickly stripped through the school of bait. A strike will usually come immediately and will literally tear the rod from the angler's hand if he is not holding it firmly. If the first angler is successful and hooks a fish, the driver then has a chance to cast to the same area, this time allowing the line to sink before stripping it in. Usually a salmon or two will still be around where the bait-feeding flurry occurred to take any crippled herring that remain.

If either angler is successful, the fight from these feeding-frenzied fish is unmatched. Long runs and sky-reaching water-walking leaps are the norm. When finally boated, it is questionable whether the fish or the angler is the most tired.

It is important to understand the sequence that occurs if the angler is to have consistent success. Whatever factors cause the salmon to start feeding usually also excite the bait-herring into feeding on small zooplankton which is their feed. The coho will literally herd the herring towards the surface using the surface as a check on their movement and escape. When the herring have reached the surface and are most congested, the coho slash through them grabbing as many as they can in their mad rush and crippling many others with their tail as they dart through the school. Once the bait school has been scattered, the coho circle many times through the cloud of herring scales, striking any crippled and erratically swimming herring that remain. When satiated, the coho sound and rest while they digest what they have eaten. When the feeding urge occurs again, they search out another school of herring which they can corral near the surface. Gulls use this symbiotic relationship, assisting the coho by diving at the bait-herring as they near the surface, further concentrating the bait until the ball is tightly compacted.

For the angler the key to success lies in watching gulls and interpreting when they have seen a ball of bait which is accessible to the boat. The action at its peak usually lasts only a minute or so, and it is necessary to speed to the edge of the herring ball before they are scattered. On occasion I have watched a herring ball and its subsequent feeding flurry of coho and gulls last for upwards of five minutes, but that is rare.

The specific times fish feed will usually occur on a daily basis, especially if a run of coho is migrating through a particular area. When is a matter of local knowledge; it could occur in early morning, late evening, or at any time during the day. Tides, weather, and bait-fish are the key factors.

Usually I look for feeding schools of coho at the beginning of the day, then after the furious actions calms, I search for bait schools of herring which have moved to shelter near a kelp bed or, hopefully, in the shallows.

Some of my most memorable fly fishing for coho has occurred along very shallow beach areas where bait fish have been forced to school because of intense predation by feeding salmon in deeper waters.

These shallow feeding areas are very few and your success will depend upon the salmon migration and size of herring. Usually the young herring of the year concentrate in the shallows during mid–July through August. Prior knowledge of these specific areas is helpful but they are not difficult to locate. Just cruise the beach areas near kelp beds and look for small schools of bait fish which are obviously holding in a specific area. As always, success demands that there be actively feeding coho in the vicinity. However, this is one of those rare times when solitary coho can be the rule. These single predatory fish can often be seen slowly swimming under the bait fish — which in turn signal that the predator is there by parting the school, leaving an open zone immediately above the coho. It is literally a cat–and–mouse game as the coho will leisurely swim under the bait schools and then suddenly dart forward to snap up a single herring, which for whatever reason has exposed himself to the feeding instinct of the coho.

Fly fishing in these circumstances creates an adrenalin high which is often difficult to describe. When fly fishing shallows, I slowly boat into the area — often in water so shallow that I must raise the outboard motor and drift in to where I will anchor. Even knee deep water is capable of offering superb fly fishing. However, I have found that a wading angler, no matter how hard he tries to stay still, will spook feeding fish. The boat, however, offers the advantage that the angler is higher and can cast farther, thus extending his stripping reach. Boats moving in the vicinity do spook the coho, however a stationary boat does not appear to frighten the salmon away.

Once anchored, I have had my best success with a pink minnow fly, a shrimp pattern, or a pink bucktail with the keel hook cut off, leaving just the trailing hook. The bucktail fly has, surprisingly, offered an incredibly exciting addition to this fishing. On this fly I have had smashing strikes which literally bounced the free fly line off the bottom of the boat and zipped it through the rod guides before I could even think of setting the hook. Truly, it is this smashing strike that makes me search out shallow water fly fishing as the ultimate experience with open water salmon. One of my most memorable strikes occurred while I had a tape recorder on in the boat. Later, when I timed the screaming reel, I found a full 25 seconds of non-stop running on the first strike of that particular fish. When he stopped, the fly line was long gone and I was well into my 300 meters of braided nylon backing.

Depending on the beach area you are fishing, depth will determine whether you use a sink-tip line or a full wet line. A slow strip retrieve is the real secret to this fishing. Usually when the strike comes, the line stops abruptly, often with the fish showing near the surface with mouth open as he tests this strange food. This kind of strike provides ample opportunity to set the hook, but be prepared: when the fish feels the pull, he will make a sudden mad dash for deeper water, peeling slack line from the boat floor which will hit the reel in a sudden screaming protest.

I have found that shallow water beach fishing is best during full flooding or ebbing tides. On one particular area where I fish each summer, coho will move on the small bait herring schools only on the ebb and only when there is a constant northeastern wind. Ideally there should also be a plankton bloom offshore into which the bait herring can escape. These conditions will exist only a few times during the summer but fly fishing is supreme when conditions and fish coincide. In all fairness though, I must say that the action is often slow with strikes occurring only after many casts.

Should the action be particularly slow in the shallows, use the flooding or ebbing tides or other key times to search for coho along protruding points. These areas exist in many locations throughout the Straits of Georgia and are usually characterized by having an offshore kelp bed with land dropping rapidly into the sea on one side. These are prime feeding areas for both springs and coho and usually harbour large schools of bait fish in and around their kelp beds or at the drop offs.

Fly fishing from these areas is usually done from an anchored position near the end of the kelp bed or in a specific position along the side of the kelp bed, where feeding salmon are known to concentrate. These areas of concentration are usually easy to locate by the constant action of small feeding gulls. They hover over the area where salmon have chased the bait fish near the surface away from the kelp.

Having found one of these points with a kelp bed,

anchor or tie to one of the kelp fronds. As the tide begins to run, try to cast with the running tide to stretch line and fly to the fullest length possible. After the cast, let the sink tip line lie, allowing the running tide to straighten it before beginning the retrieve. One of my favourite areas lies off the reef south of the Cape Mudge lighthouse opposite Campbell River. This area is good only during a racing ebb tide. In fact, the water rushes by so quickly that it is often difficult to anchor. However, it is a most effective area during the summer months for feeding coho and often a number of anchored boats can be seen in the area.

Generally I use two basic retrieves for all salmon fly fishing. I am certain there are others and I'll continue to search for them because the *retrieve* is truly the key to success! The first retrieve is the standard short strip, jerking the fly in short-timed strips through the water. The second is the almost nymph-like retrieve which will move the fly ever so slowly through the water. I have tried a rod–under-the-arm two-handed speed retrieve, but have yet to have any real success with this method. I do feel, however, that it has potential, for we know that motor bucktailing the fly is most effective. I have also tried tying the leader to the head or body of the fly in an attempt to create a crippled action, but — again, I had only limited success.

Experimentation, as the reader can gather, is one of the real appeals to open water salmon fishing. Successful flies can be easily determined by motor bucktailing if the angler is in need of confidence for particular patterns or colours. But consistent success must come from proper retrieves, which coastal anglers still need to perfect.

It was during my early years of experimentation that I discovered the very slow nymph retrieve with standard sinking lines and floating lines. At that time I was searching the open waters off Cape Lazo for bluebacks, the small, under five pound coho which frequent the area in May through June. These coho exist in large schools near the surface, feeding primarily on shrimp larvae. Schools of small pink salmon also frequent the area, often mingling with the bluebacks.

On what was to be a most memorable day, I had spent at least an hour cruising the open waters in the vicinity of the Comox–Powell River ferry route before I located feeding salmon near the surface. The main school seemed to be located around a several hectare–sized floatsam concentrated by a light wind and a tide rip. I could see the occasional blueback leaping and surface feeding on shrimp. The salmon were travelling in what appeared to be small schools adjacent to this debris. My floating line was ready and when I stopped the boat, I took a few false casts and then dropped the fly near surfacing fish. I was still using the strip retrieve at that time and spent the next half hour in utter frustration, changing flies, speeding the retrieve and cursing the uncooperative trout-like surfacing salmon.

Finally, I cast the line out and decided to leave it and have a cup of coffee. The fly floated just below the surface and I twitched it lightly as I drank from the thermos cup. A fish struck! After letting the fly rest again — it was a bright red fish-hair body, pink hackle pattern — I then moved the line ever so slowly. Another strike. This time the fish was hooked, and I brought in a three pound blueback. By now I had the idea and soon two additional beauties were lying in the fish bucket alongside the first. Since then, I have used this slow retrieve technique throughout the year with varying success.

In May and June, searching for schools of bluebacks is the only successful method I have found for finding these salmon. This often means miles of wandering the open waters of Georgia Strait before a school is found. Naturally, it requires calm waters, but these are the norm in the Strait at that time of year. A school is usually located after sighting a concentration of gulls feeding on surface shrimp larvae. I have also found that young pink salmon will often be in the same area. These take the fly just as well as the small coho, but they are nowhere near the fighters they will be when in estuaries of rivers late in July through August.

For the novice at open water salmon fly casting, the ideal classrooms lie at the mouths of the various North Island rivers like the Adam-Eve, the Cluxewe, or the Keough. Here, beginning late in July, small schools of pinks begin to arrive at the mouths of their home rivers. Fly fishing can be from a boat or wading from the shore and if pink salmon are showing, success is virtually certain.

The fish are easy to locate, often leaping as they cruise along the shallow beaches or porpoising with just their backs showing as they surface to taste the stream water right in the estuary. All rivers have what can best be termed a 'PINK' pool; a tidal pool where pinks hold for a short time when they first enter the river. Such pools, when located, provide a true bonanza for the casting fly fisher.

Casting for pinks has the added bonus of hooking the occasional coho, and on rare occasion, a spring salmon which might be cruising the estuary at the same time.

For pinks, I use a silver-bodied fly with red tail and red streamer, which I have dubbed the Pink Eve because of the success I have had at the mouth of the Adam-Eve river. It remains my favourite for all seasons. Another good pattern is the Pink Glennis. The retrieve for pinks is a very slow strip, similar to the blueback retrieve and their take is like the coho, a sudden halt. However, pinks, like whitefish and grayling, have a soft mouth and care must be taken when the hook is set and during the fight.

One major challenge still remains for the open water salmon fly fisherman: to create a fly and find a retrieve which will consistently take chinooks. These are the fish of deep water, early mornings, and sunset evenings. They are often taken on a trolled surface bucktail and therefore must be susceptible to a cast fly. They will take various fly patterns in streams, among them a silver-bodied, bright blue streamer which I have found to be particularly successful in fresh water. But what is that special retrieve and under what conditions will they take consistently in open salt water? A perplexing challenge indeed.

XVIII
The Elusive Searun Cutthroat

by Tom Murray

By Steve Carter
03/28/85

"Here today and gone tomorrow." This phrase might have been written with the Searun Cutthroat (Salmo clarke clarke) in mind.

I have spent fifteen years trying to learn a little about these elusive creatures, often without much success. I have learned something of the type of place they inhabit, the tides they appear to like, a type of gear that works well and various other bits of information which I shall endeavour to pass on to you.

I think by now I have fished every month of the year for searuns but my favourite time is the fall after Labour Day. The beaches tend to be quieter then, and the air has that wonderful snap to it. Often the days of September and October are windless and calm. A rush and a surge in the water behind a quickly retrieved fly can stop your heart and make you tremble; we call it "beach fever". However, I remember vividly a June day of bright sun, moderate breeze, one to one-and-a-half foot waves and my first fish of over twenty inches.

Cutthroat like a gently sloping beach rather than a quick drop-off. An old rule of thumb for a good cutthroat area says,

"Rocky beach, good slope, three bi-valves (mussels, oysters, clams, etc.) and eelgrass."

A tide chart is the cutthroaters' bible, as this will indicate the best times of day to fish. Generally, cutthroat seem to prefer a good mid-tide changing to flood, although some beaches do produce on a falling tide. I often find that casting to a piece of drifting kelp or flotsam will produce results. The reason for this is what appears to be one of the favourite foods of the searun — the stickleback. The small schools take refuge from sea birds and fish alike by hiding under this floating debris and a fly placed just off the edge and retrieved with a short jerking motion could yield a fish or three.

A little story goes with this casting to kelp and floating debris. A few years ago, again on a club fishout, six or eight of us were lined up casting to what seemed a no-fish day. I was casting to a piece of kelp out about forty feet from shore when suddenly, after three or four casts, I was into a fish. I released it and cast again — another fish! I released it and cast again. Another fish! This time I backed out and let one of the other members into my spot. He cast to where he thought I had been casting but missed the kelp by a few feet. After a few minutes, which seemed like hours, he moved out and I returned to "my spot". First cast and you guessed it. I had another fish! I think I caught six or seven fish that morning just off that piece of kelp.

As you work your way through your cutthroat apprenticeship, you may get to sense the good days — the "cutthroat days". I don't quite know how to describe the feeling — rather like a sixth sense — you just know the fish are there. Over the years I've asked other cutthroaters if they have ever experienced this feeling. To my surprise, they all admitted there was "something" one seemed to sense if it was going to be one of those days.

It is most important to **stop** — slow yourself down, take time to **look** — try to see what is happening, and **listen** — it is amazing what you can hear. On approaching a beach, it is wise to stop and look, visualize and remember — where are the creek channels, the large boulders, the eel grass and kelp beds? — are there any fish moving? — is the ride ebbing or flooding? — is there feed in evidence? — are there any other fishermen on the beach? — have they caught anything? I learned a long time ago not to rush into the water and just start casting. On my first-ever fishout with the Totem Flyfishers of B.C., I was a little too eager. While the experienced cutthroaters stood on the beach checking for the above signs, I waded out about thirty feet and began casting. A shout from shore brought me up short — the fish were chasing feed about twenty-five feet *behind* me.

As far as gear is concerned, there is no perfect combination. My cutthroating friends use everything from Hardy cane rods to the latest in boron. I would, however, strongly recommend one of the salt water or new graphite reels. Please, please, please, save yourself the agony I suffered when I used a Hardy "Princess" for a couple of outings. The salt water will ruin a reel such as this very quickly, no matter how well you wash it or try to protect it.

I have tried sink tips, slow sink, high float, medium float, double taper, level, weight forward, etc., and have found what I think is the ideal, almost perfect line — Northern Line Company's "Ultimate Plus" Floating Light line. A Canadian product, it is 110 metres long with a 20 metre head, the rest is running line or backing. An excellent floating line, it casts like a darn with one or two false casts.

My own gear is either a nine foot Scott PowrPly or nine-and-a-half foot Winston Graphite rod with a Berkley or Marryat reel and the floating "Ultimate Plus" fly line. Rod, reel and line are all a six-weight system. I've tried rods from three-weight to eight-weight. The #3 is only good in a flat calm and the #8 has just too much power for cutthroat.

Leaders are a special topic. I make my own. I like long leaders, twelve to eighteen feet, and this is what I use for both cutthroat and interior lake trout fishing. Any good leader, your own or store bought, about nine feet long will work but make sure your have a .008 (4 lb.) tippet and take along lots of spare tippet material. The 4 lb. tippet is ideal for a size twelve fly but on occasion you will require larger flies and being able to change tippet sizes quickly keeps you fishing.

You know, fly fishing need not be an expensive sport. With a little checking at the local department and discount stores, I know I could buy a reasonable fly casting outfit for under $100.00 and still have lots left over for a few flies.

Probably the most important part of your gear is the fly you use. My favourite fly is the Rolled Muddler. When I

Rolled Muddler.

started cutthroat fishing, there were a few popular local flies like the Golden Mallard, Coachman, the Professor, the Muddler Minnow and the polar bear hair flies in all their different colours and sizes. The Knudsen Spider was a favourite of the

Washington cutthroaters as well as many other patterns, including dry flies.

The "Rolled Muddler" is one of those flies that evolved because I was looking for a pattern that imitated our local salt water beach stickleback. The fish is quite small, about one to one-and-a-half inches in length, has a silver-white belly, speckled sides and a greenish blue to brown back. The natural mallard flank feather was chosen for a wing because, after trial and error, it was consistantly the most successful. A coloured "wing" on the fly such as blue, green or brown just did not get as many hits. Because size was critical and I was retrieving just sub-surface, the best hook choice was the Mustad #9671 size 12 streamer hook. It isn't too small to miss a strike and it isn't so big that it is difficult to remove from a fish. Because the "cutts" look up at the fly as they do most food near the surface, I concentrated on getting a shape that fished well and didn't roll or bellow out as some streamers and bucktails do. To get the stiffness and outline I wanted, I folded or "rolled" the natural mallard flank feather for the wing and tail. Silver mylar was the answer for the body. I added a reverse rib to hold it all together and I had the basic pattern. I wanted a flat-sided, bullet-shaped head and this was achieved by using spun deer hair and trimming it. By using red tying thread, I could get a little gill colour by trimming the hair to the hook shank on the bottom. By leaving three or four longer hair strands along the body, I got the lateral line. It is not difficult to tie, but I like my flies sparse, and I often go back and reclip until I feel the fly looks right. It was an instant success for me and has been responsible for many of the best days I've had cutthroat fishing. The retrieve I use when fishing this fly is very important. When I saw those stickleback darting in the six to ten inch movements that are characteristic of this bait fish and started retrieving with a quick wrist action that I thought imitated the fish, I had my system.

I don't vary this very much when I'm fishing for searuns, as many of my friends will tell you. I'm always looking for something better but this system really seems to work. Consider the following:

It was a day in late October; a beautiful B.C. fall day; a cutthroat day. My fishing partner and I decided to work the rising tide as our first choice.

As we arrived at our starting point after catching the first ferry, we realized we were the only cutthroaters out that weekend. It didn't matter. It wasn't raining and it looked as though we might have a little sun. Perhaps a perfect day. Little did we know!

As we often do, my partner and I discussed patterns, rod length, line weights; the usual sort of patter cutthroaters seem to mumble. We decided to try a new fly I had used with some success for pink salmon on a trip to Port Hardy earlier in the fall.

As we approached the water, we saw a fish move about thirty feet out. The tide has just turned. After two quick false casts used with a quick jerking retrieve, my partner was into the first fish of the day. I don't know how many searuns we hooked and released that day but we had never had a day like it before. It was almost a fish a cast. They ranged in size from twelve to perhaps twenty-six inches. We had never caught as many two pound plus fish. We were as giddy as a couple of kids in a candy store. We were missing fish we should have landed. We didn't care — next cast, another fish. It seemed to last all day. That was one day we won't forget. Oh, yes — I went back the following weekend — nothing!

I suppose to be successful at this type of fishing, it helps to have good old-fashioned intuition and experience. However what really is important for success is to just get out and do it. I've had many fine hours with good friends on the beaches and like all other cutthroaters, I'm still looking for that fish of all fishes — a fall "yellowbelly" over five pounds that takes me well into the backing. And yes, if I landed it, I'd release it. I haven't killed a searun in many years. In my mind, they are one of the most beautiful fish found in our coastal waters.

XIX
Night Fishing — The Quiet Time

by Alf Davy

The most peaceful time to fish is at night. To be on a lake or in moving water as the day comes to a close and the stars appear is a very special feeling.

I can remember hearing stories of how fish do eighty or ninety percent of their feeding at night. Does it not make sense to fish at night when the fish are feeding? Certainly, you will not have to stand in line for your favourite fishing spot.

My first introduction to night fishing came in New Zealand in the late 1960s. I had spent a day fishing a lake and was packing up to go when a couple of fishermen arrived from Auckland. After exchanging some pleasantries, they then asked why I was leaving so early. They informed me that I would miss some good fishing by not going out at night. I was easily persuaded to give it a try and rowed out in front of the camp to a shallow bay. Following some advise, I had a great couple of hours that night with a fish on almost every cast.

In my travels about New Zealand I met other fishermen who were going fishing at eight or nine at night. Most of them felt it was the best time to catch fish.

I thought I had struck gold and could hardly wait until I got home to take advantage of this secret way of catching fish. To my great disappointment, whenever I tried night fishing in the Pacific Northwest, it never seemed to work. Yes, I could catch fish with dry patterns on nights when the fish were taking sedges but I had no success with wet flies.

It was not until a few years ago when I was able to spend a year in Taupo, New Zealand, in the late 1970s that I was able to go back to night fishing. I again studied how to fish at night and this time I looked for the little things that made it work.

One of the first things I was told was that you did not go out to fish when there was a moon out. There were some nights when I wanted to fish and I did not really believe them. As it turned out they were nights when all I did was practice casting. I had thought that the moon would help the fish find the insects, but of course the insects knew this, and they, unlike me, stayed at home.

I know that when sedges hatch, the fish will turn onto them, and moon or no moon, you can have some great fun. I knew a group of Kamloops fishermen who used to work shifts and they would go out after midnight when the sedges were hatching. For me, though, my best sedge fishing was on moonless nights or when clouds covered the moon.

In New Zealand most of their night flies were large and dark so I thought the fish must be eating large things. At home, fish eat small things so when I came home I fished with my best shrimp, mayfly and chironomid patterns. But again it did not work very well.

In desperation I tried larger leech patterns and finally had some success. It was more important that the fish could see the larger fly in the profile of the night sky than it was to match any hatch.

All Black.

When I go night fishing I try to find a shoal area, near deep water, that the insects and the fish will move onto at dark. Large shallow bays will also afford good night fishing. The best fishing will be the last fifteen minutes before dark. I always take a flashlight in order to change flies. Never shine the light in the water. I did that my first night in New Zealand while landing a fish and I had to wait a good thirty minutes until the other fish came back.

The best leader to use at night is one to two meters with a minimum of an eight pound tippit. There are two reasons for this. A short, stiff leader has less chance of tangling or of breaking. You do not want to waste valuable fishing time untangling line or tying on new flies.

The best retrieve is a slow one. But you must be willing to try all speeds. One night I was fishing without much success using a sinking line and thought I would try my All–Black on a dry line. After a dozen casts without any success I decided to go back to my wet line and started to bring my line in very fast. I hit a fish! In my next hour, I had constant action on a fast retrieve.

D'Mouse.   Tom Thumb.   Muddler.

When sedges are hatching, it is the easiest time to experience success at night. I fish a large deer hair pattern like D'Mouse, Muddler or large Tom Thumb to attract the fish. I usually cast towards the lighter sky as I have more chance of seeing the fish take. Otherwise I must go by sound or feel. One has to be prepared to cast in the general direction of where the fish are moving.

Streams are just as good as lakes for night fishing, especially for brown trout. A couple of years ago I found that I could take browns by floating a small dry fly down stream then retrieve it up in the surface film. I had many fish on the drowned dry fly coming upstream. A large deerhair fly brought upstream with lots of splash will attract trout. Good fishing can especially be found where small streams enter lakes. The best fishing will be found at the edge of the fast and slow water.

A word of caution — do not just walk into unfamiliar water. Always use care and a wading staff to test the bottom.

In night fishing as in any other kind of fishing, the fish can turn off as quickly as they come on. Once the fish move off the shoal, they become less available and the good fishing will stop.

For me night time is a special time to fish. The stars and sounds of night contribute to a peacefulness and solitude that are hard to capture during the day. Sometimes it does not even matter if the fish are not there.

CAVERHILL NYMPH

Peter. Caverhill

XX
A Complete Angler

by Peter Caverhill

A *complete* angler! Is it possible for such a creature to exist? What would a person be like in order to qualify for this illustrious title? Perhaps this angler would be capable of accurate hundred foot casts under any conditions. Perhaps he would have a superb acuity of sight, spotting fish where all others have failed. Or perhaps he would breast the toughest currents, tie the tiniest flies and always be first on the best water. Surely the *complete* angler would number his daily catch in the dozens as a testament to his skills. Those parts of an angler that make him eligible for the title "complete" are difficult to define. Consider the following tale.

It is one of those late summer days when haze hangs over the city and the air is hot and still. Miles to the east, away from the airborne residues of autos and factories, a little stream tumbles out of the mountains. Motivated by gravity, it splashes noisily between sun-warmed granite boulders and spreads more quietly across a broad riffle. The air between the stream and the dark green canopy of leaves is a-buzz with summer insects. Occasionally a bird flutters down and then is gone, back to some tree-top perch. Across the stream, reclining against an old downed cedar, is an angler. His mouth moves slowly, savouring an egg sandwich, while his eyes intently consume the river and its happenings. Lunch time on a summer stream alone is the perfect time for thought. His mind reflects.

The morning had been generous and he had captured a number of good trout. This success was partly due to his few years of apprenticeship under the scrutinous attention of the old man, a master at deceiving fish and teaching lessons. Then there had been many forays to a variety of fishing waters, sometimes alone, but mostly with other companions. As skills evolved over the past half decade, there had been many fish dinners and a few of them had filtered, forgotten, to the bottom recesses of the home freezer. Their later appearance and deposition to the garbage can would twinge his conscience. These days he kept few fish, despite a penchant for their delicate taste and the generosity of the rules. From time to time, like this morning, he would keep a fish and it would become the focus of a celebration to the freshness of nature and the quality of the stream. Quickly killed, cleaned, and carefully stored in a cool bundle of stream-drenched mosses and ferns, the trout would ride home with the angler to be wondered at and appreciated by his family.

The warm noontime sun felt good and the angler lay back against the mossy cedar and closed his eyes. This day on the stream, and a bit of shut-eye, was important. The evening before had been a tough one. He had attended a public meeting to represent the society's and his own interests. A new subdivision was planned and part of it would seriously affect some tiny cutthroat streams that fed a slough near his home. The meeting was well attended by local residents and agents for the developers. The tone of the meeting was strongly in favour of the plan as it stood. When it came time to discuss the environmental issues, he had tightened up his courage and raised his hand. At first his proposed changes to the original plan produced some disgusted comment from the audience, which didn't help the knot in his gut. As he explained further about the values of streams and fish, the tenor of the audience visibly started to change. At the meeting's end, he was

144

invited to be part of a committee which would favourably work out the problems with the cutthroat streams. A number of people had cornered him after the meeting and kept him going with questions until nearly midnight. He was glad that he hadn't gone into this meeting cold. He had learned all he could about this development and over the past two years, he had made an effort to find out more about fish and their requirements. He had searched out and developed contacts in a number of government agencies whose decisions affected fish and streams.

A cloud drifted across the sun and the angler's eyes snapped open. It was time to fish again. On the corner run, there was bug hatch in progress and trout were going crazy. The angler was slowly working his way downstream toward the hot spot when a middle–aged fly fisher appeared from the streamside bush, and, with a wave to the angler, made a beeline for the trout. Anger drenched the angler and he almost shouted a string of obscenities at the interloper. Sanity prevailed, and he slowly reeled in and made his way the short distance downstream to the newcomer. Politely but firmly, he explained to the stranger that he had intruded. The new–comer listened, his demeanor teetering between angry recoil and embarrassed reproach. The calm and friendly tone of the angler won out and the newcomer yielded — his ego unbruised. He agreed with the angler and apologized, explaining that, while he fished a lot, he had never really understood how anglers were supposed to sort themselves out on a stream. They parted as friendly acquaintances, with the angler describing directions to a fine run further down–stream. A society card, complete with telephone contacts, was carefully tucked into the newcomer's vest pocket and a committment had been given to attend a meeting.

Later in the afternoon, a cool mountain storm blew up in the valley and the angler decided the day's fishing was over. It had been a good one. For the trudge back to the car, the angler pulled a large plastic garbage bag from his vest. The unsightly plastic and aluminum litter, left by those less car–ing, offended him. It was easy to pick up what lay on the path back, and this material would more appropriately be dis–carded at home.

Complete Angler? As the foregoing tale implies, being complete as an angler should require going beyond the skills needed to consistently catch good fish under difficult circum–stances. Knowing tackle and techniques is important, but going the further distance is equally important, if not essential. New anglers may be excused if the first few years of their development is totally consumed with getting the line out and pulling the fish in. However, the time comes — soon — when new anglers must join with their more experienced associates and become sensitive to concepts that will ensure the continuation of nice waters in which to find fine fish. Let's look at some of these concepts.

An Angler's Responsibilities

Angling is a serious distraction. It has the power to absorb us from our early youth right through to the feebleness of advanced age. Angling, as recreation, has been a force during all of the history of modern man. Its future will depend on how seriously we view our responsibilities toward maintaining it.

Not long ago, when Model T's bumped roughly over paths that were the major routes, fishing water was abundant. When one fishery was exhausted by overfishing or industrial impact, there was always another just a little further over the next hill. In the 1980's and beyond, with expanding road systems and modern equipment, an increasing population of anglers with more free time can reach every water. Lake and stream areas important for fish and angling are shrinking — displaced by a variety of development. More anglers are having to fit into less water than ever before.

As anglers, we are going to have to shoulder the responsibility of ensuring our future more than we have ever done before. This means that we will have to give more of ourselves in return for the opportunity to have good fish and angling areas. Also, we will need to define much more precisely what is important to us in terms that non-anglers can understand. With a clear description of our requirements and a resolve to work, we should be able to convince many of those who compete for our space that we are important.

We may think that governments can ensure that our fishing needs are provided. After all, we pay them our taxes and they are responsible for environmental protection and fishery management. We should be able to sit back and let them do the job. This is true, and it would be nice, but it isn't reality. It never will be! Governments are vexed by inadequate budgets and they are pulled in all directions by people with a variety of motives. Governments need strong and constant direction from us. They are not unheeding or unbending and our efforts will produce successes. The key is the time we put into achieving what we want.

Respect for the Fish and the Environment

Having respect for fish and their surroundings should be an important condition of going fishing. Appreciating the beauty of a fish and the experience that this creature provides for us are expressions of respect. Fish should not be the sole object of our fishing efforts but, more importantly, they should be considered a bonus that adds to a wonderful time on the water.

Having respect also means that we should care about the welfare of fish — as individual animals, as populations and as complete species. We hold the life of a captured fish in our hands. To kill the fish or to release it is a decision that we should never take lightly. Many factors will influence our verdict. What do the regulations allow? Is the fish wild or of hatchery origin? Is it needed or highly desired for food? If we opt to take the fish, it should be killed humanely and its meat cared for so that it will provide a proper feast. If release of the fish is the plan, then we must take care to capture it quickly so it won't become exhausted. We must keep it in the water and handle it as little as possible while the hook is removed. Proper tackle is essential for this process. Using a single barbless hook will facilitate hook removal without causing damage. On deeply-hooked fish, it is usually best to sacrifice the hook by cutting the leader. (The hook is not likely to hurt the fish). Landing nets are essential for boat anglers and those who fish waist-deep in streams. They allow the fish to be held quietly in the water while the release is done. Exhausted fish must be held until they regain strength and composure. Most fish carefully handled and released will survive. A small number will die in our hands or later. We should keep this fact in mind if we find ourselves in a catching bonanza. By releasing a fish, most anglers are expressing their concern for the future. However, by releasing many individuals from a fragile wild fish population, an angler may be killing more than he thinks — or wants.

An enjoyable fishing experience depends largely on the surroundings. Beautiful scenery and uncrowded conditions are elements that add importance to a fishing area. Litter, in the form of bottles, bait cans, beer tabs, candy wrappers and other junk, is offensive. Many of us are passionately angered by the large deposits of refuse that we see in our favourite areas, but, we are less than careful about discarding the smaller items that seem insignificant. Lunch wrappers, bottle caps and plastic cigar ends are examples of the tiny items that quickly accumulate and reduce the good feeling of being in a clean natural area. It's easy to tuck personal bits of refuse into a pocket for later disposal back home. Refuse control soon becomes an automatic response. From time to time, take a garbage bag in your vest and clean up after those who have gone before. It's sometimes messy, but you will feel good, and those coming later will appreciate your respect for the area.

Angling Ethics

Ethics are rules of conduct devised by people who are involved in an important social activity — like angling. Ethics are usually the product of many years of development. Sometimes they are written down for all to see, but often they are simply passed along by the more experienced members of the group to the neophytes. Fishing ethics are like this, and it can be difficult for a new angler to determine exactly how his peers expect him to behave on the water. An angler who violates the traditional rules of conduct, either with intent or unknowingly, can set off a whole range of emotions in other anglers. Tempers flare, arguments occur and no one has fun.

Years ago, the rules that anglers devised to sort themselves out on lake and stream were not very different from what is in place today. However, fishing waters used to be uncrowded and adherence to these rules was less critical than it is today. With areas getting more heavily fished each year, it is essential for new anglers to learn what is expected of them. Equally important is the need for the experienced types to re-examine their understanding of angling ethics and to actively educate those less knowledgeable.

The boat angler who anchors too close to others, who runs too close to areas where people are fishing or who motors to and from a crowded shoal at high speed is not being ethical. A stream angler who "hogs" good water and will not move downstream, rotate, or share the water after having good success is not being ethical. These are some obvious examples of poor behavior, among many others that we must try to avoid. After all, angling is an activity that should emphasize contemplation, relaxation and recreation — not competition, tension and ulcers.

Respect for Other Anglers

For many of us, fishing is a way of life. Years are spent acquiring the skill and the knowledge that is necessary to consistently find and catch good fish. Some of us are attracted to certain ways of fishing. We are bait chuckers, spoon slingers, fly fishers and float fishermen. Our deep emotional involvement with fishing and the methods we use means that we are often secretive, suspicious, jealous and competitive in our relationship with other anglers. These are qualities that often produce friction between different types of anglers. This is unfortunate, and like poor ethics, can make the fishing experience imperfect.

We need to try to understand other anglers and to communicate with them on a regular basis. This doesn't mean giving away all of our hard-won secrets. It does mean working together for the common purpose of ensuring that we will always have fish and nice places in which to go fishing. Anglers at each others throats only make these important goals less attainable.

Skillful and ethical anglers should be respected, despite their tackle persuasions. Beginners, who are stumbling along in a new activity, also need our help and regard. Respect for other anglers really means appreciating different viewpoints and trying to shape or change the outlook of those less knowledgeable or less caring than we are.

Taking, Giving, and Being Effective

The first few years of becoming an angler are concerned with learning skills, trying waters and catching fish. For many of us who survive the initial difficulties and discouragements, fishing becomes a pretty serious distraction. Even when we aren't actually out on the water, we are frequently thinking or talking about fishing. It is a very important part of our existence.

Despite the mark that fishing makes on our lives, few of us earnestly commit time to ensure that our way of life will continue. The future of fishing will depend on anglers acting together. After years of taking from our recreation, each of us should be looking for ways to give a little back. What should we do? How should we do it?

Join an organization. Get together with other anglers who feel the same as you do about fishing. There is certainly strength in numbers and a group which speaks on an issue forcefully, intelligently and rationally can command a lot of respect and attention.

There are a number of groups available for the individual to join. Some of these are aimed solely at conservation of important fish stocks and preservation of quality fishing. Others mix social (having fun) objectives with conservation. Depending on the availability of organizations in your area, you are likely to be most effective by joining more than one. It is logical to be part of a local fishing club (which will work on local issues) and also be part of a larger organization that concentrates on important special interests — like steelhead. Outside of the groups with fishing orientation, there are many other associations whose activities will affect our important fisheries. Citizen advisory groups that deal with land use planning are very important for anglers to infiltrate and provide a strong case for fishery protection. The essential thing in joining any organization is that you be prepared to spend some time working on the important issues. This will be your most effective contribution.

Groups don't always run smoothly. A mesh of different personalities can produce disagreement and friction and the group may get off track for awhile. This is normal, but it reduces effectiveness. Remember that a group with purpose and structure always has the potential to be effective. It can always be steered back on course again by those who are not caught up in the squabbles.

Become knowledgeable about fish. You don't have to get a degree in biology but learn about the life cycles and important habitats of fish in your area. Be familiar with the types of activities that seriously affect fish and their habitat. Know the basics of how fish and recreational fisheries are managed. This knowledge will give you an ability to determine which issues in your area may have impact on your fishing.

Know who the key players are and what their jobs entail. Most often these people will be government employees who work as planners and resource managers in local, provincial and federal government agencies. Make contact with your town planner, area fisheries biologist, forest manager, water engineer and mines inspector. These people cannot know of your concerns unless you tell them. Also, these people can provide you with considerable information on their area of responsibility and on issues that concern you. We anglers have a penchant for picking up rumours about a variety of things, especially pending environmental carnage. We get upset and sometimes go off in the wrong direction. Talking to the managers will help us to decide if what we heard on the grapevine is serious and requires further action. It is a wise individual or group who keeps a written directory of important contacts.

Be optimistic! There is always lots to get down about, and certainly we won't win every battle to protect our fishing. However, pessimism breeds more of the same. It's a disease that easily spreads and reduces our capability for being effective.

After all that striving to be an accomplished fisherman, you now know that there's more to it than hundred foot casts and many fish days. Think about the past. Think about how quickly things have changed — how fast the future is coming and the changes that it will bring. Now you know how important it is to become more than just "an angler". Be a "COMPLETE ANGLER".

XXI
What are you using?
B.C. Patterns

by Alf Davy

As one of the most common questions asked, it is also the most difficult one to answer honestly. Since patterns and names mean very little, it is better to determine what colour and size. Most flyfishers I know will tell the colour and size of the fly.

Flyfishers are often thought to be a secretive lot and not prone to giving out information, but beginning fly fishermen must appreciate the time and effort that can go into developing patterns. Sometimes you get lucky with a pattern and on the first try it comes together and is great. But in most cases, it takes years to get the pattern right. For example, Jack Shaw of Kamloops has spent thirty years developing some of his patterns. Can you expect someone to give away all that time and effort easily?

For the "Gilly" it was a major problem to get B.C. patterns which in many cases, represent years of development. I felt the effort was needed because my own growth as a flyfisher was dramatically changed when I was given the fly box of a very good flyfisher to study. I did not copy these new patterns but they started me in a new direction of matching the insects of our Interior Lakes.

Once I became proficient I could then offer other flyfishers an exchange of my knowledge for theirs. In this manner there is growth in flyfishing and the exchange of ideas can help develop the unique styles and methods of our B.C. fishing. Instead of relying on other areas for our information we can develop our own.

It is in this spirit that the following flies are illustrated. They are a guide which I hope others can develop further. Although someone may feel a pattern or one similar is his, there are very rarely any new fly patterns.

The patterns listed here are those used by flyfishers I have known or been in contact with while compiling this book. The tying methods and origins are as close as possible to the way I found them. They are presented as a guide for others to become better flyfishers and sportsmen and to create the cycle of giving something in return. An extension of this idea is to return the fish themselves for others to enjoy.

Chironomidae

Tunkwanamid

Golden Peacock

Moose Mane

Little Black

Long Black

Black Hackle

Yellow Copper

P.K.C.K.

Green Gold

Hatheume

Chironomidae

Editor's note:
Many chironomid patterns now have initials as names. My experience is that, when asking fellow flyfishers what chironomids they are using, they usually answer by colour, trim and size. I am calling the patterns as flyfishers use them (except some original patterns).

Tunkwanamid:

Hooks:	8 to 16
Tag:	Silver tinsel
Body:	Peacock with silver ribbing
Gills:	Optional with white acrylic or emu
Data:	One of the original chironomid patterns of B.C. by Tom Murray of Vancouver.

Golden Peacock:

Hooks:	10 to 14, long shank
Body:	Brown or gold peacock with medium oval gold rib
Thorax:	Peacock built up with extra wrap, grouse feathers tied shellback
Data:	Good fly for chironomids; may also be fished in larger sizes just under the surface as sedge pupae.

Moose Mane:

Hooks:	10 to 14
Body:	3 or 4 strands of moose mane or bell wrapped along body of fly. Try to have one lighter colour strand to imitate segments.
Thorax:	Grouse tied in at one–quarter of fly and then tips of feather are tucked down under front to simulate pro–legs.
Gills:	White acrylic may be used; tie under wing case.

Little Black:

Hooks:	10 to 16
Body:	Black floss, tying thread or poly. The fly should be tapered slightly towards the front (thicker at front) — fine silver or gold rib.
Thorax:	A couple wraps of green gold acrylic with white acrylic at front for gills.
Data:	The standard chironomid pattern.

Long Black:

Hooks:	8 to 12, long to extra long shank
Body:	Black floss or tying thread — fine silver or gold rib
Thorax:	Grouse feather tied in one-quarter of the way back and then lighter tips of feather tied down under eye of hook, one-half way to hook point at most
Gills:	White acrylic yarn at top of fly.

Black Hackle:

Hooks:	10 to 14
Body:	Black floss or tying thread tapered towards front — fine silver or gold rib
Thorax:	Grouse feather one-quarter of way back to front
Hackle:	Small black hackle tied sparse
Data:	May be used in surface film as well as deep water

Yellow Copper

Hooks:	10 to 16
Tag:	Silver tinsel
Body:	Light yellow yarn with fine gold or copper ribbing
Thorax:	Yellow seal, a few wraps tied very loosely.

P.K.C.K.:

Hooks:	10 to 14
Tag:	Silver tinsel
Body:	Green yarn with stripped peacock quill
Thorax:	Light brown turkey tied at one–quarter and up to eye. Body under thorax is darker colour than body
Gills:	Piece of emu or white acrylic or ostrich herl at either side of eye
Data:	Early B.C. pattern by Powell, Kilburn.

Green Gold:

Hooks:	10 to 12 long shank
Body:	Green, gold acrylic (imitates peacock) with fine copper wire ribbing, tapered towards eye of hook
Gills:	White acrylic tied on top.

Hatheume:

Hooks:	10 to 16
Body:	Green poly with fine copper wire ribbing
Thorax:	A couple of wraps of peacock herl
Gills:	White acrylic or emu wrap behind eye of hook
Data:	Fine copper wire not only adds weight to the fly but enhances the segmentation.

Copper Brown

Pheasant

Blood Worm

Red Butt

Dry Flies

Humpy

Lady McConnel

H.C.H.

Tom Thumb

D'Mouse

Muddler

Copper Brown:

Hooks: 10 to 16

Body: Brown poly or yarn with fine copper wire ribbing. Body is tapered towards the eye.

Gills: White acrylic or ostrich herl at eye.

Pheasant:

Hooks: 8 to 16

Body: Three or four strands of pheasant tail wrapped from bend of hook to eye

Thorax: Pheasant rump tied one–quarter shellback and tips brought forward and then folded down under eye. Tips should be no more than one–half way to tip of hook.

Blood Worm:

Hooks: 8 to 14, regular and long shanks

Body: Dark red or maroon yarn body, fine copper wire ribbing

Hackle: 6 to 8 strands of pheasant rump wrapped on sparingly

Data: Jack Shaw of Kamloops was one of the first in B.C. to use this pattern.

Red Butt:

Hooks: 10 to 16

Tag: Bright red yarn

Body: Dark brown pheasant tail, a few strands wrapped along hook with wide gold tinsel ribbing

Thorax: A couple of wraps of peacock herl

Gills: White acrylic yarn or white ostrich

Data: A favorite fly of Brian Chan of Kamloops.

Dry Flies

Humpy:

Hooks: 10 to 14, fine wire

Tail: Deer or moose hair tied in as part of hump back of fly

Body: Grey sparkle yarn. The tips of deer hair or moose are tied in at bend of hook. They are then twisted into rope and layered over the back of the fly as a hump. This gives the fly its floating quality.

Hackle: Black hackle at front

Data: An excellent chironomid dry pattern developed by Jim Crawford and Alf Davy for Hatheume Lake.

Lady McConnel:

Hooks: 10 to 18, fine wire

Tail: Light grizzly hackle tip for tail

Body: Grey poly body, deer tied full/shellback for floatation

Hackle: Light grizzly hackle

Data: Tied by Brian Chan as a dry chironomid pattern for the Kamloops area.

H.C.H.:

Hooks: 10 to 16

Body: Green and gold acrylic sparkle yarn to imitate peacock colour. Deer hair is then layered over back of fly to form a tail hump back and some bristles at the eye.

Data: Stands for Hatheume Chironomid Humpy and was developed for guests at that Lodge.

Tom Thumb:

Hooks: 8 to 16, fine wire

Tail: Deer hair ends

Body: Deer hair is tied in at the tail with butt ends. The thin ends of the deer hair are pulled forward to form a "sheath" body and tied off at the head. Deer hair is then spread up or around to form a hackle. Light grizzly hackle can be added as a variation. If you use thicker tying thread for this fly it can be more durable. You may tie it up from bend of the hook to get better hooking qualities.

Data: The major dry fly of British Columbia Lakes from sedges to tiny chironomids.

D'Mouse:

Hooks: 6 to 10, long shank

Tail: Optional deer hair at tail

Body: Spun and clipped deer hair cut to tubular shape around hook shank. You may, as an option, dub in any body colour of seal. Most of the time natural deer hair is fine.

Data: Developed by Alf Davy in early 1970's for a durable floating pattern.

Muddler:

Hooks: 4 to 10, long and extra long

Tail: Mottled brown turkey

Body: Solid gold or silver tinsel wrap

Hackle: Deer hair to point past bend of hook

Wings: Brown mottled turkey wing

Head: Clipped deer hair — rounded

Data: Canadian pattern by Don Gapen

Notes on Fly Fishing

Blue Dun

Deer May

Baetis Dun

Canadian Sedge

Shrimps (Scuds)

Little Guy

Doug's Drifter

Werner Shrimp

Seal Shrimp

Anderson Stone

'52 Buick

Blue Dun:
Hooks: 10 to 14, fine wire
Tail: 6 to 12 elk hair tips
Body: Iron blue sparkle yarn
Top: Elk hair post with grizzly hackle tied parachute (four turns)
Data: Tied by Brian Chan of Kamloops to represent Callibaetis Mayfly Dun

Deer May:
Hooks: 10 to 16, fine wire
Tail: A couple of strands of fine hackle
Body: A bundle of deer hair with yellow wrap
Top: Deer hair post with a few wraps of grizzly

Baetis Dun:
Hooks: 14 to 18, fine wire
Tail: Very fine strands of hackle, long and thin
Body: Creamy white synthetic dubbing
Hackle: Grizzly hackle tied parachute–fashion around deer hair post
Data: An effective representative of the Baetis Mayfly dun

Canadian Sedge:
Hooks: 6 to 10
Tail: Red or green
Body: Grey wool with green rib
Wing: Barred Mallard breast feathers
Hackle: Grizzly hackle
Data: One of the first sedge dry fly patterns in B.C. Tied by Col. Carey for Beaver Lake.

Shrimp (Scuds)

Little Guy:
Hooks: 8 to 12
Tails: Hen pheasant or grey parts of male tail feather
Body: Light green, olive or dark green seal is dubbed and spun on body. The tail is tied down first, then the seal is picked out of the bottom to represent the legs of the shrimp.
Data: One of the best trolled or cast lake patterns on shrimp.

Doug's Drifter:
Hooks: 8 to 12
Body: Brown or light green blended yarn. Part of the material extends back of the hook bend and is wrapped tightly with matching tying thread. It has ginger hackle palmered on the lower front half
Data: Tied by Doug Porter for Roche Lake in Kamloops.

Werner Shrimp:
Hooks: 8 to 12
Tail: Deer hair
Body: Olive seal is dubbed on, then ginger hackle is palmered on. The deer hair is then tied shell–back over the seal
Data: Mary Stewart of Vancouver originated the fly. The name is associated with Warner Schmid of Vancouver.

Seal Shrimp:
Hooks: 8 to 12
Body: Olive seal is dubbed and spun on body of fly. Top is then clipped close on top and the bottom is picked out to simulate legs of the shrimp
Data: The simplest pattern for the novice to tie and catch fish with.

Anderson Stone:

Hooks: 8 to 12 long shank

Body: Cream yellow yarn on lower body with brown tied shellback. Black tying thread criss–crossed over yarn. Brown hackle palmered to front and trimmed short and uneven.

Data: Originated by Earl Anderson of Vancouver for Harrison River cut–throat. A good general river pattern but also used for a variety of lake fish foods like the shrimp.

'52 Buick:

Hooks: 8 to 12

Tail: Light yellow

Body: Various shades of green seal but olive is the most popular

Ribbing: Medium oval silver or gold

Beard: Yellow to point of hook.

Head: A few wraps of peacock herl

Data: Originally tied as a damsel fly nymph by Gary Carlton of Edmonton. Today it is tied mainly as a shrimp or dragon pattern.

Notes on Fly Fishing

Nymphs

Pennask

Fullback

Halfback

Peacock Nymph

Caverhill Nymph

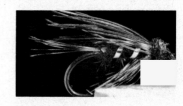

Doc Spratley

Knouff Lake Special

P.D. Pupae

Kamloops Pupae

Interior Sedge

Nymphs

Pennask:

Hooks:	8 or 10, long shank
Tail:	Pheasant rump
Body:	Peacock with fine oval silver or gold ribbing
Legs:	Stiff peacock eye, 2 or 3 to each side
Wing:	Pheasant rump — the dark red are best
Data:	Tied in the late 1960's for Penask Lake by Alf Davy. Excellent trolled or fast stripped pattern.

Fullback:

Hooks:	8 or 10, long shank
Tail:	Pheasant rump
Body:	Peacock herl. Pheasant rump is tied shell-back over the peacock.

Halfback:

Hooks:	8 to 14
Tail:	Sparse pheasant rump
Body:	Peacock herl tapered towards the eye. Pheasant rump is tied in halfway on fly and laid over thorax with tips of feather folded under as beard.
Data:	One of the most versatile and effective B.C. patterns. If tied thin and small, it is a chironomid; if a little larger, a mayfly or damsel and on very large hooks, a dragon.

Peacock Nymph:

Hooks:	8 to 12
Body:	Peacock herl
Thorax:	Peacock eye (dark blue) is tied shell back
Legs:	Some of the fronds from the peacock eye are left and folded back to the side as legs
Data:	When tied small, it is a chironomid pattern; when larger a nymph pattern.

Doc Spratley:

Hooks:	6 to 12, long and regular shanks
Tail:	Sparse grey or partridge hackle
Body:	Black yarn with silver or gold ribbing. It is also tied in almost any body colour.
Wing:	Pheasant tail or rump feather
Throat:	Grizzly hackle tied down as beard
Head:	Optional peacock herl
Data:	Fly originated by Dick Prankard. One of the most famous trolling flies in use in B.C. Waters. Depending on the size, it can imitate most of the major insects as well as leeches.

Caverhill Nymph:

Hooks:	8 to 16, long shank
Body:	Black mohair wool
Rib:	Silver (flat or oval)
Hackle:	Black or dark blue
Head:	Herl-type synthetic wool
Data:	Tied by Peter Caverhill in early 1970's. It is used in B.C. for trout and steelhead as it represents many different food items.

Knouff Lake Special:

Hooks: 6 to 10, long shank
Tail: Orange golden pheasant tippit
Body: Olive chenille tied thick with yellow ribbing
Hackle: Soft blue–grey pheasant rump tied back and sparse
Data: Very good pattern when fish are in the shallows feeding on sedge pupae. Use a sink tip or weighted pattern with a dry line.

P. D. Pupae:

Hooks: 8 to 12, long shank
Body: Olive seal or olive chenille with copper wire ribbing
Thorax: Grey feathers of small inner pheasant tail tied half back with tips tied under or to the side
Data: Use on a sink tip line or floating line in the shallows and on a sinking line in mid–water to imitate sedge pupae. Use prior to and just after hatches.

Kamloops Pupae:

Hooks: 6 to 10, long shank
Body: Medium to light olive with stripped peacock on front half. Green or grey pheasant rump tied half back on top. Tips are tied under as beard
Head: A few wraps of peacock herl
Data: A good sedge pupae in smaller sizes and dragon nymph in larger sizes. Original pattern by Jack Shaw.

Interior Sedge:

Hooks: 6 to 10, long shank
Body: Medium to light olive seal
Thorax: Brown Seal
Wing: Duck quill cut to shape at both sides and golden tippit as beard
Data: Excellent sedge pupae or dragon nymph pattern. Original tied by Jack Shaw of Kamloops.

Notes on Fly Fishing

Black O'Lindsay

Carey Special

Fastback

Squirrel

Yellow Fullback

Palmered Fullback

Skinny

Des Roche Nymph

Corixa

Stump Damsel

Black O'Lindsay:

Hooks:	6 to 10
Tail:	Brown and blue hackle fibers
Body:	Yellow yarn or seal with gold ribbing
Hackle:	Brown and blue mixed
Wing:	Peacock sword with gray mallard over top.
Data:	One of the most popular attractor patterns for Canadian lakes

Carey Special:

Hooks:	4 to 10, long shank
Tail:	Groundhog hair
Body:	Groundhog hair with black silk thread
Hackle:	Two or three pheasant rump feathers
Data:	Originally called "Monkey–faced Louise". Dr. Lloyd Day of Kelowna found a groundhog on his fishing trip and asked Coloney Carey to tie a fly from the hairs. Today it has many body colours and is usually tied with pheasant rump.

Fastback:

Hooks:	8 to 12, long shank
Body:	Black yarn, brown yarn or peacock
Wing:	A thin, long piece of black or brown marabou. It is tied so that it extends well past hook.
Data:	Excellent pattern fished with a very fast retrieve.

Squirrel:

Hooks:	8 to 12
Tail:	Squirrel
Body:	Black or dark maroon yarn
Hackle:	Squirrel tail
Data:	A very good pattern when fished with a fast retrieve.

Yellow Fullback:

Hooks:	10 to 20, regular and long shank
Tail:	Yellow hackle
Body:	Yellow yarn with pheasant feather tied down as shell back with yellow thread over back
Thorax:	Slight hump of pheasant feather
Hackle:	Yellow hackle tied under as beard.
Data:	Tied by Brian Chan

Palmered Fullback:

Hooks:	8 to 16 regular and long shank
Body:	Peacock with ginger hackle palmered along fly. Pheasant tail is tied shell back over top.
Data:	Old favourite in the Kamloops area.

Skinny:

Hooks:	10 to 18
Tail:	Sparse grizzly
Body:	Peacock, very thin. Thin pheasant rump as shellback, tied over with tying thread as rib for support.
Hackle:	Grizzly hackle very thin as beard.

Des Roche Nymph

Hooks: 10 to 14, regular and long shank

Tail: A few strands of ginger hackle

Body: Cream to tan dubbed rabbit fur ribbed with flat gold tinsel and turkey tail tied shellback

Hackle: Ginger hackle tied under as beard

Data: Tied by Brian Chan of Kamloops as a callibaetis mayfly nymph.

Corixa:

Hooks: 10 or 12

Body: Light yellow yarn with strand of silver tinsel along bottom. Turkey wing feather is tied over body on top with a strand of feather out each side at middle.

Data: Pattern originated by Jack Shaw.

Stump Damsel:

Hooks: 10 or 12

Body: Green Phentex yarn with yellow thread as ribbing

Thorax: Peacock with ginger hackle palmered and turkey feather tied over at top

Data: Refer to chapter in book for history.

Notes on Fly Fishing

Bottom Walker

Gomphus

Hatheume Nymph

Rat Lake Special

Leeches

All Black

Blood Leech

Split Leech

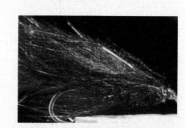

Rabbit Leech

Bent Leech

Rolled Muddler

Bottom Walker:

Hooks:	6 to 10, long shank
Body:	Deer hair is spun on and clipped to shape of dragon nymph. Olive is dubbed on body or coloured felts are used for desired colour.
Thorax:	The dark blue of the peacock eye is tied over the top of the thorax and a few strands of peacock are left out each side to imitate legs
Hackle:	Black moose mane is tied down as beard past hook point
Data:	Pattern developed by Alf Davy in early 1970's. It can be walked slowly along bottom weeds to imitate a dragon nymph foraging for food. The deep hair body and moose hackle will keep it generally weedless.

Gomphus:

Hooks:	8 or 10, long shank
Body:	Spin deer hair on hook, clip to shape of dragon nymph (gomphus), leaving a good gap at hook point
Legs:	A few strands of hen pheasant tail
Head:	Spun deer hair clipped round
Data:	Developed by Jim Crawford in late 1970's to imitate gomphus dragon nymph. It is best in natural deer hair but may be coloured with felts. Fish slow on the bottom.

Hatheume Nymph

Hooks:	8 to 12, long shank
Body:	Insect green or grey chenille with wide gold, silver or copper wrap.
Hackle:	Soft blue–grey pheasant tied sparse. (Must be blue–grey)
Data:	Tied at Hatheume Lake Resort and is one of the best all–purpose patterns. In large sizes it can represent a dragon nymph, in medium sizes a sedge pupae or in small sizes a shrimp pattern.

Rat Lake Special:

Hooks:	8 to 12
Body:	Grey chenille with yellow or orange chenille at head
Hackle:	Pheasant rump spun sparse
Data:	A favourite attractor pattern at Hatheume Lake.

Leeches

All–Black:

Hooks:	6 to 10, long shank
Tail:	Black Marabou
Body:	Deer hair spun body clipped close to hook shank. Black seal is dubbed over deer hair
Wing:	Marabou tied in two or three clumps along body. Black moose mane tied long as beard past hook point to keep hook free of weeds.
Data:	Originated by Alf Davy. A very good leech and general night pattern. Fly can be retrieved slowly on bottom with few hook–ups.

Blood Leech:

Hooks:	6 to 10, long shank
Body:	Brushed out maroon and black yarn (or blended seal). Tie it in clumps along body and then with a fine hairbrush, brush the fly
Head:	Red thread
Data:	An exceptional leech pattern made famous by Jack Shaw.

Split Leech:

Hooks: 8 and 10

Body: Two hooks are tied tandem. Barb is cut off front hook (regulations). The rear hook is tied with spun deer hair, then clipped close and dubbed with black seal. Front hook is weighted with fine fuse wire and dubbed with black seal. Black marabou is tied in along front hook shank.

Data: The front of the fly will sink and the rear will float; it will undulate when retrieved. Very good mid–water pattern.

Rabbit Leech:

Hooks: 6 to 10, long shank

Body: Black chenille

Wing: A strip of black rabbit along the back to the end of the hook.

Bent Leech:

Hooks: 6 to 10, long shank

Tail: Black marabou

Body: The hook is bent up about half way up the hook. Fuse wire is added to front half and the body is dubbed over with black seal

Data: An excellent leech pattern for mid–water as it gives an undulated motion in water

Cutthroat

Rolled Muddler:

Hook: 12 streamer

Tail: Natural mallard flank feather

Body: Silver mylar, rib of silver, reversed

Wing: Folded or rolled natural mallard flank feather

Head: Spun deer hair trimmed. Red tying thread behind and in front of head. Two or three stands of deer are left along the body for lateral line

Data: Coastal cutthroat pattern tied by Tom Murray of Vancouver.

Notes on Fly Fishing

Steelhead Flies

Telkwa Nymph

Black Stone

Telkwa Stone

Skunk

Davie St. Hooker

Thompson River Rat

Pete's Lady Bug

Black Woolly Worm

Steelhead Flies

Telkwa Nymph:
Hooks: 2 to 8
Tail: Goose flight feather
Body: Back half is black seal and front half yellow seal with a gold or yellow ribbing
Thorax: Turkey wing is tied over yellow front half and ginger hackle is palmered on lower half. A pair of brown quills are tied forward.
Data: A favourite fly of the Maxwell's Lodge on Bulkley River.

Black Stone:
Hooks: 4 to 8
Tail: Goose quill
Body: Black yarn or poly with peacock ribbing
Thorax: Dubbed seal with quill over back and turkey wing trimmed short out the side. A small quill is put back out to each side.
Data: Tied by Dennis Clay.

Telkwa Stone:
Hooks: 4 to 8
Tail: A goose quill out each side.
Body: A bunch of deer hair is wrapped along hook shank with orange thread. The deer hair must stick out past the hook bend.
Wing: Deer hair long on back and clipped short on front. Another pair of goose quills are placed forward on each side.
Data: The dry fly used by the Maxwells at their camp on Bulkley River.

Skunk:
Hooks: 2 to 8
Tail: Scarlet red
Body: Black chenille with silver ribbing
Hackle: Black as beard
Wing: White polar bear hair.

Davie St. Hooker:
Hook: 2 to 8, long shank
Tail: Hot pink fake fur.
Tag: Silver Tinsel
Body: Fluorescent bicycle flasher
Wing: Goat hair and hot pink fake fur
Beard: Polar Bear hair
Head: Red
Data: Tied by Ehor Boyanowsky of Vancouver.

Thompson River Rat
Hook: 4 to 8, long shank
Tail: Deer hair dyed green or bucktail
Body: Spun white Caribou hair with furnace grizzly hackle palmered along body
Wing: Long thin green sparkle yarn or fake fur
Head: Red
Data: Tied by Ehor Boyanowsky as a variation of the Miramichi Bomber.

Pete's Lady Bug:

Hooks: 2 to 8, streamer
Tail: squirrel
Body: Dark brown body, hot orange hackle is palmered along bottom and salmon chenille is added on top as shell back
Ribbing: Silver oval tinsel
Head: Red
Data: Excellent pattern for Thompson steelhead. Tied by Pete Peterson of Vancouver.

Black Woolly Worm:

Hooks: 2 to 8
Tail: Red Fluorescent yarn
Body: Black chenille with long grizzly hackle palmered along the fly
Ribbing: Silver oval tinsel

Notes on Fly Fishing

Thor

Squamish Poacher

Stillaguamish Sunrise

Fall Favourite

Salmon Flies

Pink Eve

Butler's Red and White

Butler's White

Green Herring

Thor:

Hooks:	4 to 8
Tail:	Orange hackle or orange yarn
Body:	Dark red chenille
Wing:	White bucktail or polar bear hair extending to end of tail
Hackle:	Optional mahogany saddle hackle tied down as beard.

Squamish Poacher:

Hooks:	2 to 6
Tail:	Few strands of orange bucktail
Body:	Orange chenille with orange hackle palmered (longer at back). Orange surveyor tape is tied down over the tip and two glass eyes are tied in.
Data:	Fly is creation of Joe Kambietz of Vancouver, B.C.

Stillaguamish Sunrise:

Hooks:	2 to 8
Tail:	Mixed yellow and red hackle
Body:	Yellow chenille with silver tinsel
Hackle:	Yellow orange
Wing:	White Polar Bear.

Fall Favourite:

Hooks:	2 to 8
Body:	Silver Tinsel
Hackle:	Scarlet
Wing:	Hot orange

Salmon Flies

Pink Eve:

Hook:	1 or 2 Dubin point Mustad–Limerick hook, forged T. up looped oval eye black.
Tail:	Fluorescent light pink fish hair
Streamer:	Same as tail
Body:	Wrapped mylar tinsel #10, (other tinsels not as effective)
Thread:	Fluorescent pink nylon.
Data:	The following salmon flies were tied by Barry Thornton of Vancouver Island.

Butler's Red and White:

Hook:	1, 1/0 or 2/0 Superior Mustad-O'Shaughnessy hook, stainless steel forged ringed
Streamer:	Polar bear hair with a strip of fluorescent red fish hair
Thread:	Metallic silver or pink.

Butler's White:

Hook:	as for Butler's Red and White
Streamer:	Polar bear hair
Thread:	as for Butler's Red and White.

Green Herring:

Hook:	as for Butler's Red and White
Body:	Wrapped mylar tinsel #10
Streamer:	fluorescent green pink hair
Thread:	Green, with eye painted on head.

Notes on Fly Fishing